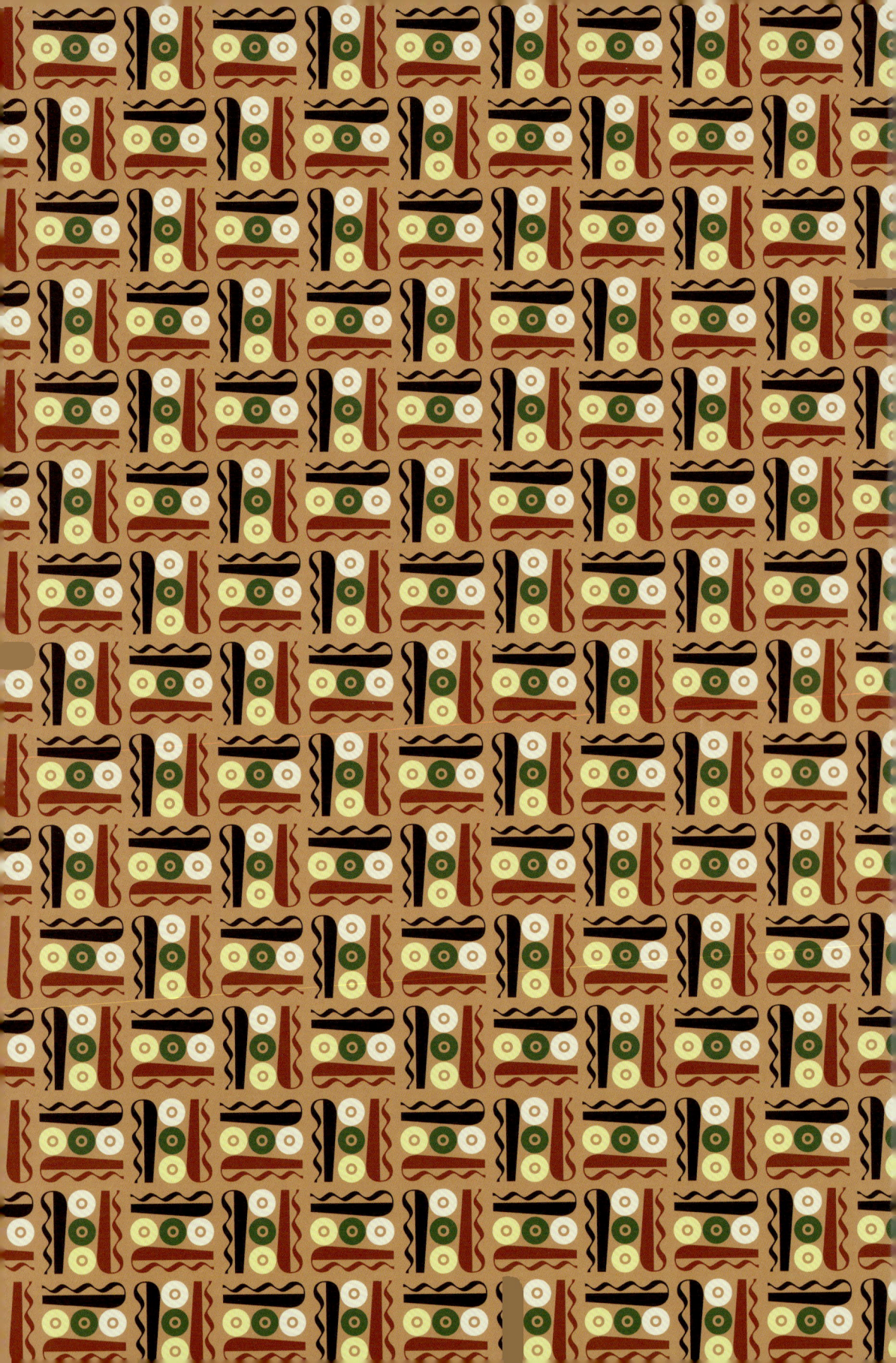

BERTHOLD
WOLPE

BERTHOLD
WOLPE
THE TOTAL MAN

PHIL CLEAVER

INTRODUCTION This book is a celebration of Berthold Wolpe and brings to life his story through anecdotes from friends and family giving us graphic insight into what it was like to know this larger than life character. ¶ Berthold Wolpe was a curious man; I mean he was filled with curiosity. He spent his life packing his brain with ideas and knowledge and his home with all sorts of '*things*'. As a designer he was a true original; as a person he was a charming, humorous, quietly-spoken man, invariably decked out in trade-mark deerstalker hat and cape, who made people smile. ¶ Berthold was a master of calligraphy and type design, a prolific dustjacket artist and polymath, who had a magpie curiosity for collecting any-thing that would fuel his creative world and inform his design practice. ¶ It takes interesting people to produce interesting work, and Berthold's love of life fed his design practice. ¶ Berthold's work has been reproduced extensively, especially many of the 1,500 front-cover book designs he created at Faber & Faber. However what has not been shown before is all his lettering, hand drawn on scraps of paper with white correcting paint refining the hand drawn black lettering. They show the process of creating the energetic and strong letter forms which he made his own. ¶ These artworks carry the human touch in their design, an element so evidently missing from our computer-generated age where graphic design is becoming increasingly surgical and sterile. These artworks open up a bygone era of design and will hopefully inspire young designers to close their laptops and get messy with paper and ink, producing work which carries their own DNA and not that of the computer.

Frontispiece Berthold in his early twenties living in Germany. Opposite Berthold in characteristic hat and coat outside Faber's photographed by Frank Herrmann, who worked there.

Opposite Berthold's father Simon Wolpe, seated in the foreground, in the forest where Bethold's grandmother owned and ran a sawmill and a chain ferry.

Left Berthold and Hilde's father, Simon Wolpe (Artist not known).

Right Berthold's sister, Dr Hilde Wolpe. Painted by Joan La Dell, who lived next door to the Wolpe family in Walton Street in the 1950s.

Bottom Berthold's painting, from memory, of his Grandmother's sawmill on the Baltic Coast of Prussia, where he would spend his summers as a child, along with his many cousins.

GAZETTE

OBITUARIES

WOLPE had a re-
esting head, which
tracted Daumier. I
e that he was de-
Dürer — after all,
Offenbach, not so
Nürnberg.
an unusual com-
st and scholar. He
il of the great cal-
olf Koch and be-
ant. Their associa-
ted in *Das ABC-*
4), an elegant
most frivolous Ro-
c alphabets drawn

coming to Eng-
here he settled in
nvited by Stanley
ign a printing type
rs for the Mono-
on, based on let-
pe in bronze which
en.
e was cut in 1934
as titling on the
Monotype Recorder
in the summer of
led Albertus, and
elf as the most
display" face in
ny years. It was a
since it was com-
to copy or repro-
hically, and there
nt in lettering de-
en" by every sign-
ntry who had any
ed on shop fronts
ed), vans, carrier
s everywhere. If a
n paid for every
d, Wolpe would
ry rich.
r four years at the
St Martin's Lane
gham, where he
of the famous
ackets on yellow
moved to Faber
ere he remained
ent in 1975, and
signed over 1,500
bindings, as well

Wolpe read, re-
llected, not books
instruments con-
ing and measur-
g in Chelsea, he
on the pavement
house a metal in-
nt by the stall-
rgical, but which
s a pair of divid-
shed to be earlier
British Museum.
arried a leather

'MONOTYPE' ALBERTUS

ABCDEFGHIJ

KLMNOPQR

STUVWXYZ

.,!M&W&;:?

£1234567890

TITLING CAPITALS SERIES NUMBER 324

REGISTERED DESIGN NO. 811437 - 14 TO 72 POINT

Designed by Berthold Wolpe *Exclusive to The Monotype Corporation Limited* *Registered Trade Mark* MONOTYPE

Berthold Wolpe

graved tradesmen's cards, wax lucifers, a writing tablet and other memorabilia: they had been waiting some 200 years for him to identify.

In 1959 he was made a Royal Designer for Industry. Some years later he had a telephone call from *The Times* requesting him to come in and see the Editor on the

ing) in 1968, the citation included these words:

For eight years, this College was enriched by his presence as teacher of his variegated lore, and many persons here present will recall nostalgically the shy but irresistible enthusiasm with which he was wont to pull out from specially-designed recesses deep in his gamekeeper-ish garb, as it might be a pair of Byzantine scissors or a Hispano-Moorish inkhorn,

one of them. We who went to see the retrospective exhibition of his work at the V & A in 1980 expected much, but were astounded by the variety and vitality of his work.

There is an exuberance about all the different work he did for Rudolf Koch between 1927 and 1932 which overflows from all the

beautif
(used t
exhibiti
ous Ten
italic t
ston's I
ing, and
— all f
striking
seen a
House
genius
demand
that for
But
most e
work f
tween
fare Pr
great v
style. A
own. H
hand a
countle
disting
all othe
recogni
Mare's
mark
literary
One
own, a
The le
signed
with er
Like t
stantly
space
when "
very th
ieve m
nication
ter Len
If he
tering,
scholar
Reader
in 1981
fred
Handw
thority
calligr
and ed
the M
Steing
bet of
ible de
tering.
Kenni
But
miss
stood
verse.
recogn
heart,
most
When
loyal
Crow

BERTHOLD LUDWIG WOLPE (1905–1989)
Very few designers have left a pervasive and permanent mark on graphic design in the 20th century but Berthold Wolpe was certainly one of them. We who went to see the retrospective exhibition of his work at the V&A in 1980 expected much, but were astounded by the variety and vitality of his work.¶ There is an exuberance about all the different work he did for Rudolf Koch between 1927 and 1932 which overflows from all the different media, tapestry, metalwork, jewellery, enamel in which he worked. All bear the mark of his fertile and distinctive talent, most of all those that are lettered. For lettering, seen as a pattern that bears a message, Wolpe had a unique talent. When he came to England, he was conscripted by Stanley Morison to design types for the Monotype Corporation. If Albertus was the first and most famous, there were others, the beautiful Hyperion italic, Pegasus [used to good effect for the 1980 exhibition catalogue], the vigorous Tempest titling and a sans serif italic to go with Edward Johnston's London Transport lettering, and the Gothic Sachsenwald—all fine and all different. His striking hand-lettering can be seen at its best in the Guyon House Press Magna Carta, and his genius for

The Independent Obituary of Berthold was written by Ruari McLean and Nicolas Barker. Text and The Independent reproduced with permission © The Independent, 6th July 1989. Nicolas' text starts above, both are far better writers of his life than the Author, and since the book is a collection of other people's writings far more appropriate to start this portrayal of The Total Man.

devices was much in demand (a notable example is that for the Pelican History of Art).¶ But perhaps his greatest and most enduring monument is his work for Faber and Faber between 1941 and 1975. At the Fanfare Press he had done jackets of great vitality, but in the Morison style. At Faber's he came into his own. His beautiful and distinctive hand appeared in the lettering of countless jackets and covers. It distinguished Faber books from all others: it made them instantly recognisable; like Richard de la Mare's typography, it was the mark of the most distinguished literary publishing list of our time. ¶ One gift Wolpe had was all his own, and in it he had no equal. The lettering-pieces that he designed for bindings were replete with energy, grace and legibility. Like the jackets, they were instantly recognisable. In a narrow space—particularly in the war, when '*war economy*' made books very thin indeed—he could achieve miracles of allusive communication; Lawrence Durrell's *Bitter Lemons* is a notable example.¶ If he was a great designer of lettering, he was also a notable scholar of history. He was Lyell Reader in Bibliography at Oxford in 1981-82, and co-author with Alfred Fairbank of *Renaissance Handwriting* (1960). He was an authority on the great Elizabethan calligrapher Jean de Beauchesne, and edited with characteristic wit the Merrion Press facsimile of Steingruber's *Architectural Alphabet of 1773*. He had an inexhaustible delight in every aspect of lettering, which filled both his Kennington house and his mind. ¶ But we—his friends—will miss a man who, like Cavafy, stood at a slight angle to the universe. The sight of his wonderfully recognisable figure warmed your heart, with his big nose and the most beautiful smile in London. When he spoke (and he was always a loyal attendant at the Double Crown

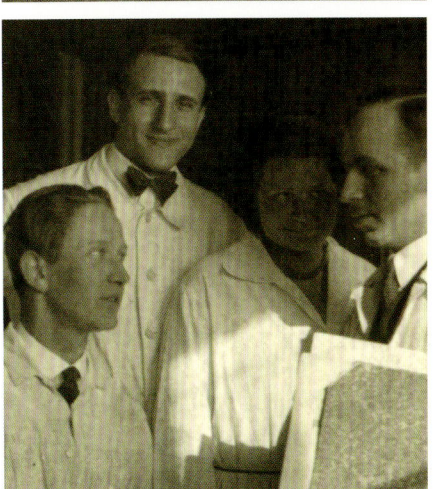

Left to Right Berthold aged 5, first day at school. Both the next two photographs show Berthold in the early 1930s still living in Germany.

Bottom left Berthold shown in the studio with his fellow workers at Koch's workshop in Offenbach, after training as a metal engraver and goldsmith in Pforzheim.

Bottom right Rudolf Koch, a family friend advised Berthold, then still at school, to undertake an apprenticeship with the local bronze foundry before going onto art school.

Top Berthold (shown fourth from the left) late 1920s/early 1930s in Koch's studio with co-workers.

Bottom Berthold with co-worker in Koch's studio.

Opposite Tapestry designed by Berthold Wolpe in 1930 and embroidered on linen in Rudolf Koch's workshop. Psalm 86:11.
Eight lines of capital letters, outlined in blue with red centre line, within red and red-and-green bars. Between the lines of lettering are seven bands of linear abstract designs in black.

Club and the Printing Historical Society) it was always with some wholly original observation. If Albertus never made his fortune, it pleased his sense of irony to find it all over the world, gigantic on Centre Point, minute on Spanish coins.
This obituary was written by Nicolas Barker

Berthold shown working in Koch studio, early 1930s.

WOLPE, BERTHOLD LUDWIG (1905–1989), graphic artist and typographer, was born on 29 October 1905 in Offenbach am Main, Germany, the younger son and third child of Simon Wolpe, dentist, and his wife, Agathe Goldschmidt. He was educated at a technical school (Realschule), as he was good even then at metalwork (through experience in his father's dental laboratory). He was expected to become an engineer, but in 1924 he went to Offenbach Art School and began his career. He worked under the great calligrapher Rudolf Koch, whose assistant he was from 1929 to 1934. Their association is celebrated in their book Das ABC-Büchlein (1934; English edition, 1976), an elegant little collection of roman and Gothic alphabets drawn by both men. He

Top The craftsmen's marks of Rudolf Koch and his co-workers—Berthold's mark is shown top row, second from the right.

Bottom Berthold shown, with Koch, practising his archery.

learned goldsmith work under Theodor Wende at Pforzheim Art School and taught in both Frankfurt and Offenbach from 1930 to 1933. ¶ In 1932 Wolpe visited London and met Stanley Morison, who was interested in some bronze lettering of Wolpe's of which he had seen photographs. Morison asked Wolpe to design a printing type of capital letters in the same style for the Monotype Corporation. This was the birth of Albertus, first cut in 1934 and used in 1935, which quickly became the most widely used display face (that is, for advertising, not books) in Britain. Its apparent simplicity made it look easy to copy or reproduce photographically, and since there was no copyright in lettering it was 'stolen' by every signwriter in the country who had any taste. It appeared everywhere on buildings, shop fronts (such as Austin Reed), vans, paper bags, and posters, and if Wolpe had been paid a royalty for every time it was used (which he should have been) he would soon have become a rich man. ¶ Wolpe, who was Jewish, settled in England in 1935, and from then until 1940 worked under Ernest Ingham at the Fanfare Press in St Martin's Lane, London. While there he was designing a lower-case for Albertus, issued in 1938, a new display face, Tempest, designed for Fanfare in 1935, a range of type ornaments for Fanfare published in his *A Book of Fanfare Ornaments* (with an introduction by James Laver) in 1939, a new text face, Pegasus, for the Monotype Corporation (cut only in 16 point) in 1937–40, and between 1935 and 1939 a series of innovative typographic yellow book jackets, printed by Fanfare, for Gollancz. He applied for naturalization in 1936, but it was not granted until 1947, and in 1940–41 he was interned in Camp Hay, New South Wales, Australia. ¶ When Wolpe returned to Britain in 1941 he moved to the

A portrait of Berthold by Charles Mozley from the 1950s.

Left to right Berthold's travel permit to leave Germany 1936. Shown with the original German State stamp and a red 'J' for Jew stamped on the inverse of the page.

Photograph of Hilde, Berthold's sister, taken by the Nazi regime. Hilde was the first woman to qualify in dentistry at Berlin University in 1920. When their father became ill, she took over his practice and supported the family. Her qualifications were not recognised in England, and so she was unable to practise here.

Hilde and Berthold shown in later years in England.

Paul, Berthold's brother, shown with his wife. He emigrated to Palistine in 1932, but was later killed during the war.

Berthold's travel permit shown again, stamped by the Nazi regime, late 1930s.

Opposite Berthold was in London when the war broke out but was interned to Australia. The letters shown are him writing to his girlfriend (later to be his wife), Margaret and her grandmother, Mrs Ringland.

Mrs E. Ring
133 Nell S...
London S...
England

PASSED BY CENSOR S.104

SERVICE
SCHREIBEN
ESTA PARTE!

...aret L. Smith
...3, 34 Linden Gardens
London W2
England

PRISONER OF WAR SERVICE
Margaret L. Smith
34 Linden Gar...
London
Eng...

TRANS PACIFIC
TRANS ATLANTIC
AIR MAIL
by Air to Sydney

PASSED CENSOR

...your can...
...Coates. I have...
...years and my mother,...
...is a British subject and a...
...are still in Lond... ...re in this
...ees from Nazi oppress... ...and we all feel
...act that we cannot do anything
...use at the moment. We still ho...

Margaret L. Smith
3A Sydney Close
Chelsea,
London, SW3

OPENED BY CENSOR

Sender: Berthold L. Wolff...

DIE GERECHTKIT LIT
IN GROSER NOT DIE
WARHIT IST GESCHLAGEN
DOT DER GLAUBEN HAT DEN
STRIT VERLORN DIE
FALSCHEIT DIE IST HOCH
GEBORN DAS DUT GOT
DEM HERN SORN O
MENSCH LAS AB DAS
DU NIT WERDES EWIGLICH
VERLORN LOBT GERECHTIHEIT

DIE GERECHTIHEIT LIT IN GROSSER NOT
DIE WARHEIT IST GESCHLAGEN DOT
DER GLAUBEN HAT DEN STRIT VERLORN
DIE FALSCHEIT DIE IST HOCH GEBORN
DAS DUT GOT DEM HERN SORN
O MENSCH LAS AB DAS DU NIT WERDES
EWIGLICH VERLORN
LOBT GERECHTIHEIT

publishers Faber and Faber, in charge of jacket design, and remained there until his retirement in 1975. For Faber, Wolpe designed many books and more than 1500 jackets and covers. While working there he also taught lettering one day a week at Camberwell School of Arts and Crafts (1949–53) and at the Royal College of Art (1956–75), and, for about the last ten years of his life, he ran a unique lettering course at the City and Guilds of London School of Art. In 1966 he was invited to draw a new masthead for The Times, which was in use from 3 May 1966 to 20 September 1970. ¶ Apart from his work as a designer (which included several other typefaces, distinguished emblems and devices, and lettering for permanent and ephemeral use) Wolpe was also an author and scholar of printing history and collector of any equipment or tools connected with writing, lettering, or measuring. He was vice-president of the Printing Historical Society in 1977. Among his books was *Renaissance Handwriting* (1960), written jointly with Alfred Fairbank. When living in Chelsea he found on a stall next door to his house a metal instrument thought by the stallholder to be something surgical, but which Wolpe had recognized as a pair of dividers, later established to be earlier than any in the British Museum. The bulging briefcase he used for carrying work to and from home was apt to be full of newly acquired treasures.¶ Whenever Wolpe rose to speak, for example at the Double Crown Club, of which he was an honorary member, or the Printing Historical Society, he always produced, with his diffident but entrancing smile, something wildly unexpected but totally apposite. He had a most striking head, with a big nose, which should have been drawn by Daumier or Dürer. It was in fact drawn by Charles Mozley in his little book *Wolperiana: an Illustrated Guide to Berthold*

Opposite Scream for Justice. Written in Berthold's London handwriting in two formats, deciding the most appropriate way to illustrate the text. Shown along with a postcard of the orignal text on a painted panel from the early 1500s. The text must have seemed very relevant in the 1930s, as it discusses the reformation of Germany between the Mainz pin Feud of 1461/62 and the spread of the southern German peasant wars.

Text translates to: Justice is in dire straits the truth is beaten dead/the faith has lost the struggle/the falsehood that is high born/the God hath told the wrath of God/O man read/that thou shalt never for ever lose faith/praise justice By Peter de Groot

Opposite Berthold shown with his two daughters; Sarah and Deborah, in Laughton, Sussex, outside a cottage they had rented for the summer.

Top Alfred Fairbank, renouned British calligrapher and designer of monotypes Narrow Bembo MT No. 294, shown with Berthold. The two co-authored the book Renaissance Handwriting: An Anthology of Italic Scripts.

Wolpe, published by the Merrion Press for his friends in 1960. This book also contains one of the best photographs of him, taken outside Faber, by Frank Herrmann, who worked there. Wolpe was made a royal designer for industry in 1959 and appointed OBE in 1983. In 1981 he was Lyell reader in bibliography at Oxford University. The Society of Designer—Craftsmen made him an honorary fellow in 1984 and the Royal College of Art awarded him an honorary doctorate in 1968. He had retrospective exhibitions at the Victoria and Albert Museum (1980), the National Library of Scotland in Edinburgh (1982), and the Klingspor Museum in Offenbach (1983). ¶ In November 1941 Wolpe made a most happy marriage with a sculptor, Margaret Leslie, daughter of Howard Leslie Smith, butcher, of Lewes, Sussex. They had two sons and two daughters. Wolpe's essential Jewishness was expressed in the closeness of his relationship with his family. He died in St Thomas's Hospital, London, after a heart attack, on 5 July 1989.
This obituary was written by Ruari McLean.

Top On Brighton beach with his children: Sarah, Toby, Paul and Deborah.

Bottom Just outside the Barbican of Lewes Castle, Sussex in late 1950s. Sarah, Berthold with Toby on his shoulder, aged two, Deborah infront with Margaret behind, Paul aged 4 with Hilde.

Opposite Sarah aged 3 with Berthold in Margaret's father's garden in Lewes, Sussex.

Celebration of the launch of The Merrion Press edition of Steingruber's Architectural Alphabet 1773, published by Sue [Mahon] Shaw and edited by Berthold Wolpe.

Left to Right
Berthold Wolpe
Shirley Tucker
John Ryder
Susan Eaton
Sue [Mahon] Shaw
Rosemary Goad (the first female director of Faber and Faber)
Charles Monteith
Monty Shaw
James Moran

Berthold signed his work with his intials **BLW**, and the Wolpe family follow suit, so as you read the anecdotes:
SCW Sarah Caroline Wolpe
DHW Deborah Hopson-Wolpe
APW Alexander Paul Wolpe [Paul]
JTW Julian Tobias Wolpe [Toby]
¶ On the photographs of the lettering shown throughout the book the initals SS appear in BLW's hand. This was an instruction to the printer that the artwork was Same Size, so not to enlarge or reduce it. These artworks were transferred photographically onto film to make the printing plates, which printed all the dustjackets.

The drawing of a key, by BLW, was used as artwork for a dust jacket. Notice the 'w' subtly slipped in on the base of the key to identify it as his illustration.
Opposite Berthold shown in his mid-forties.

SCW One Sunday afternoon in 1957 or '58, the whole family went from Walton Street, up to the City of London by bus, to look at a school. ¶ Berthold and Margaret had friends before the War who belonged to a group called *'The Mudlarks'* — they went beachcombing on the banks of the Thames at low tide, finding all sorts of objects which had fallen into the river—from all historical periods—some very interesting finds, many now in the Museum of London. ¶ After looking at the school, B and M decided that as we were there, we might as well go and have a look. We climbed down the stone steps by Blackfriars Bridge onto the mud beside the embankment, and started walking along to the next set of steps, looking out for any uncovered treasure. But when we got near, we saw that the tide was coming in, and the water had risen so that we couldn't reach the steps. ¶ We turned and started back towards Blackfriars, only to find that the tide had cut us off from those steps as well. I am sure that B and M would have thought to check the tide times if that part of the outing had been planned—but it was only a spur of the moment decision, as we were in the area. ¶ We tried to attract the attention of people walking over the bridge—but at first, they just waved back at us. Eventually, someone realised that we were trapped, and called the police. Both the City police and the River police tried to reach us—the City Police had to break into a warehouse beside the river, and clamber onto a large barge moored near to the bridge. The River Police couldn't get their motor launch in close enough to reach us because the water was too shallow, so they went back to Tower Bridge to fetch another boat. We children

Opposite Toys handcrafted by Berthold, for (and with) his children, shown on a patchwork coverlet with letterforms made from Berthold's old shirts by his daughter Deborah.

wanted to be rescued by the River Police—but by then, the youngest, Toby, was getting very upset at the sight of a rotten head of cabbage which was floating nearer and nearer to his pushchair. ¶ Just as the City Police climbed down to us from the barge, the River Police arrived back towing a shallower boat. It was very disappointing! I think now that there was probably some rivalry between the two different police forces as well. ¶ We all had to climb up a metal ladder on the side of the barge, then across the deck and out into the street from the warehouse—I don't remember who carried little Toby or his pushchair. Then we got a taxi home. ¶ There was a small paragraph about the rescue in a newspaper. Berthold was embarrassed at the thought that anyone he knew would read the article and tease him about the adventure. But I think that the surname was misspelled—so he needn't have worried!

TONY KITZINGER Berthold told me how, in 1941, on board ship returning from internment in Australia as an enemy alien, he was called to the cabin of the captain who said 'Wolpe, I understand you do lettering' and went on to send him up on deck to paint 'S.S.THEMISTOCLES' on the staves of a large barrel. ¶ Curious fellow passengers gathered round asking what he was doing to which Berthold replied 'I'm making our gravestone'. ¶ Once he said that design was really very easy; all you had to do was move all the bits around until they were in the right place.

Opposite Berthold collected many things, including variations of his name and address which arrived at his south London home. *Overleaf* An extensive collection of objects, tools of his trade, from Berthold's desk. The coloured photograph shows how every inch of his desk was covered.

Top The view from the window of Margaret's back work room in Kennington Park Road. Painted by Margaret Wolpe.

Opposite Berthold's front work room at Kennington Park Road. He had a sign on his desk that read: 'Don't Panic'.

MICHAEL WOLPE Berthold Wolpe was my grandfather's brother, Paul Michael Wolpe. He was my father's uncle, and he gave his son the name Paul in honor of his brother, my grandfather. My father too, decided to give me the name of my grandfather, but he chose the Hebrew name—Michael. There is something symbolic: Berthold have chosen the German name and my father chose the Hebrew name of the same person ¶ Berthold was for me not only family, but also a role model. I knew that he and his wife Margaret were artists, who devoted their life to their art. I knew that Berthold, despite being from a Jewish origin, had chosen to build a British family, with a very little connections to the Jewish tradition. Together with his beloved wife Margaret, he has established a new Wolpe tribe in England, and I have the feel that this decision had a deep meaning. For Berthold there was probably no point in going on wandering and suffering for this old Jewish fate. ¶ Berthold had a warm, welcoming and pleasant personality. He was a real intellectual, and his knowledge of history, art and archeology were broad and inspirational. His work in the fields of letters design and graphic designs was based on a personal style, originality and useful-functional attitude, through a deep dialogue with a long European tradition. ¶ I met Berthold three times: Twice in London and once in Jerusalem.

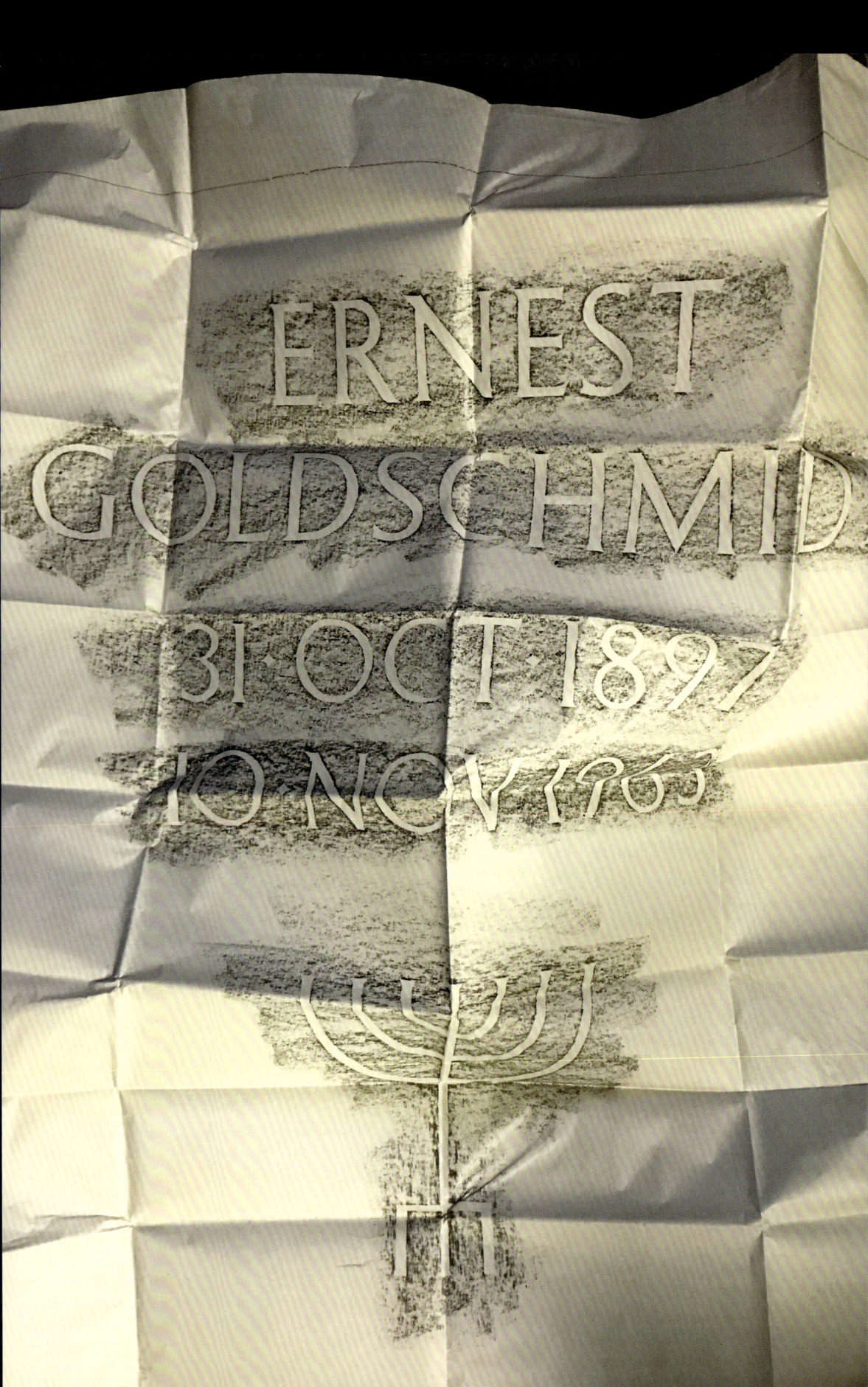

He had described to me the history of the family, told me about his immigration from Germany to England, award me some artistic perceptions, and was most responsive to my questions of my studies at Cambridge University. ¶ On our trip to the Old City of Jerusalem, he had found antiques of all kinds—quills ink and light candles, which brought to him a great joy. ¶ The almost thirty years that have already passed have not blurred the strong memory of his special character, and I thank God I had the opportunity to know him. ¶ I have to add a few words about Margaret, his wife. She was a talented painter, a family woman who I had the luck to meet many times during the months of my studies at Cambridge University. Every visit to Margaret was a fruitful experience for me. Listening to Margaret talk about her and Berthold's artistic path, her love of music, her concern for all persons in her family, the long walks with her to art markets and to music stores in London, so many wonderful experiences, I've experienced thank to her. I miss Margaret very much, and I think about her every day since we met for the last time eleven years ago. ¶ From time to time I close my eyes and a clear memory appears of Margaret and Berthold in their house in Kennington Park Road. Books everywhere, all kinds of pieces of art all over the place, the joy of being creative, and the real love they have shared between them, love that they had given in such generosity to all their many friends. Love that had filled all the spaces of the house. ¶ Through my own path as an artist, I feel as a successor of the other family members, and Berthold is one of them. Writing music today is a big challenge, and somehow I feel that my own pieces of music are connecting to Berthold Wolpe's roots.

Opposite Rubbing of a gravestone designed for his cousin.

E.M HATT In the cause of true friendship, he was manhandled mammoth printing presses up basements' steps and transported a grand piano by taxi. *'Only a box'*, he has told the skeptical driver, adding, as a jolt evoked a tinkling half-octave. *'a sort of musical box'*. Who but B.L.W., strolling homeward at 2 a.m from a bibliophiles' session, and carrying a parcel of four treasured books wrapped in *'The Times'*, could so enthusiastically have instructed the plain-clothes man in the minutiae of the books' title pages? There BLW stood, looking a pretty fair cop in his ulster and nonchalant tweed hat, a late-roaming, heavily-laden suspect, glad of an audience for one last pungent point. ¶ He loves anagrams, philological oddities, human oddities, parties, the bons mots of his own and others' children, soup-making, clockwork toys, Barbados sugar, and stopped watches (the other kind are such a menace).

BLW I didn't design Albertus as a complete alphabet, I just cut the letters needed for the bronze inscriptions. ¶ Stanley Morison, who was advising Monotype on their type production, asked me to design a printing type based those bronze inscriptions that he had seen reproduced somewhere but when it came down to produce drawings, I tried to make drawings and I couldn't draw the letters. ¶ I mean I couldn't because they were cut in the original bronzes, so I made rubbings of some of those bronzes, picked out certain letters and then prepared the drawings from those rubbings.

Opposite Original monotype letter patterns used for making matrices. Photographed by Steve Lovell-Davis. Overleaf Albertus Light originals, not used for reproduction. Enlargement showing the details of Albertus Light.

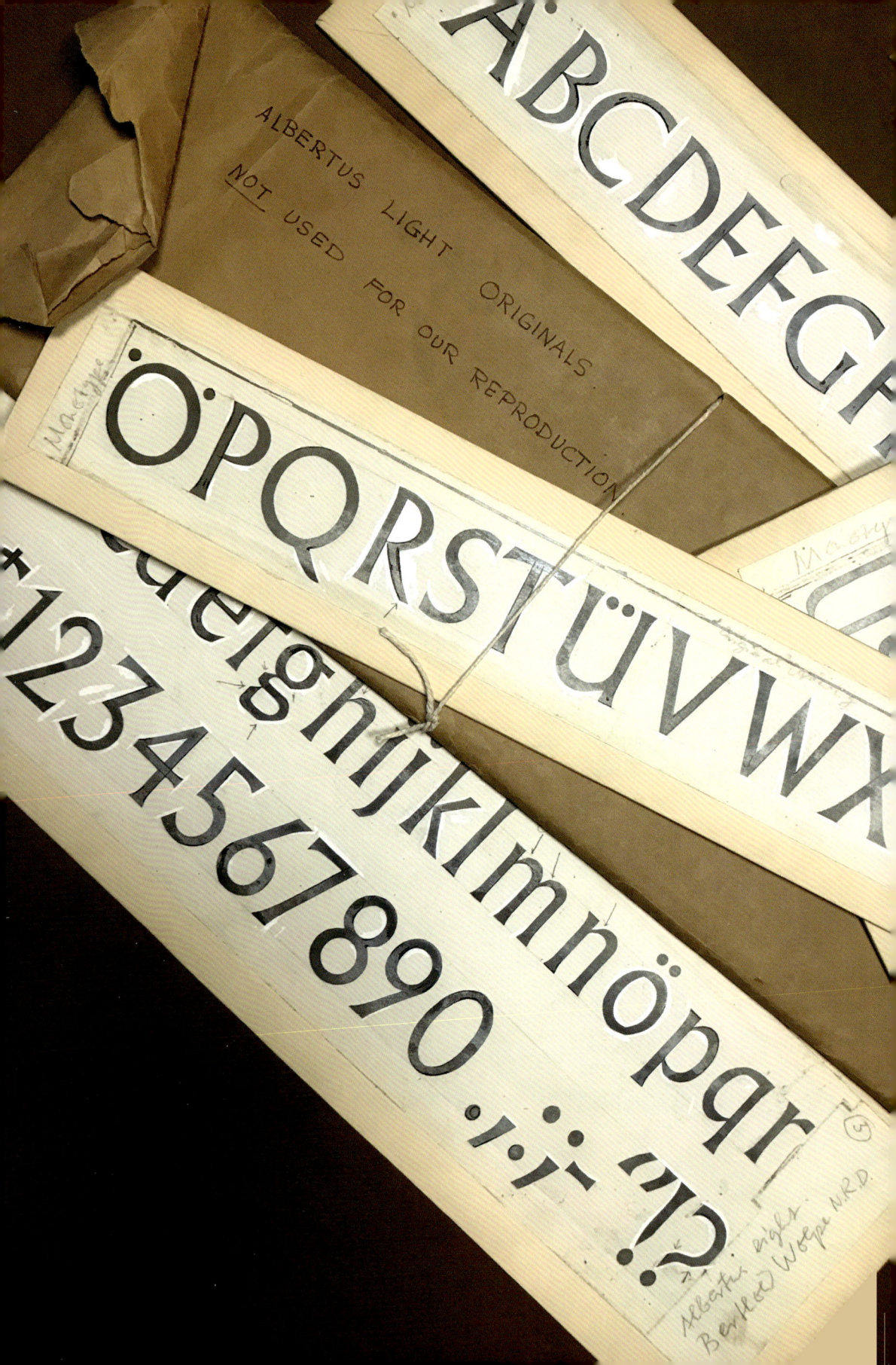

PROFESSOR DOROTHY HOGG It is always inspiring to work with individuals who have a deep aesthetic understanding of a particular craft. Berthold Wolpe was such a person, he taught me a few times at the Royal College of Art in the 1960s and I remember his knowledge and enthusiasm for lettering in all its potential forms. He was a gentle man who worked to develop an interest in lettering in jewellery and silversmithing students of my time at the RCA. ¶ I remember Berthold really well as I was interested in lettering myself. He was a serious enthusiast and he seemed quite shy as I remember, but a memorable presence and I liked and respected him, although the times were changing and I do not think there was such an interest in lettering.

Sainsbury's used Albertus for selected packaging in the late 60s. © The Sainsbury Archive, Museum of London Docklands Opposite *A proof of Albertus Bold Titling MT No. 538 60pt overlayed with 'BLW' cast by Ian Gabb at The Type Archive.* Overleaf *Tray of Albertus woodtype which belonged to his great friend, Rowley Atterbury at the Western Press. Photographed by Michael Bradley.*

ABCDEFG
HIJKLMN
OPQRST
UVWXYZ
ÆŒ&123
567890
:;-!?''

DR. IAN ROGERSON Between 1973 and 1993, as Librarian of Manchester Polytechnic, subsequently Manchester Metropolitan University, I organised an annual series of lectures on the Graphic Arts, named in honour of Stanley Morison, and sponsored by Heffers of Cambridge. The intention was to bring undergraduates and Faculty members into direct contact with celebrated practitioners. At the suggestion of Stephen Raw, Berthold Wolpe was invited to give the 1977 Lecture. ¶ At that time, I was unaware that Wolpe's paper, *Morison and Others: Reminiscences of a Type Designer*, had been widely circulated among art schools, with the result that many unexpected visitors arrived, so that a large number of students were crammed into totally inadequate premises to listen intently to Berthold's quiet voice explaining the content of his slides. ¶ When he showed an enlargement of the 50p piece with his elegant Albertus face, it was too much for one young visitor. *'How much did you get paid for that?'*, he called out. Without hesitation, Berthold replied *'One pound for each letter*'*. There were cries of outrage.

✱ DHW £1 per letter does not sound much but in 1936, £1 was about worth £50 in today's money for buying power, and Berthold was pleased to be paid at the same rate for punctuation marks as well as upper case, lower case, alternative letter forms, ampersands & numbers.

The following artworks, up to page 118, are Bertholds' original lettering and drawings. This is a small selection from the vast amounts of layouts and artworks found in the Berthold Wolpe Archive. Berthold's pencil notations on all these artworks are instructions to the block makers and printers. These artworks cover a range of lettering techniques, including: hand drawn lettering wash out lettering, brush lettering, cut out lettering, pencil letter and stencil.

the New Africa

SMITH
HEMP-
STONE

the black
reduce
risk of
lash by
1/8 of inch

S.S.
line
block

are rough
at edge
as original

5"

but sharp black please
as far as white letters
are concerned.

DHW Late one night in the 1950s, Berthold and Edwin LaDell, our next door neighbour in Walton Street, who taught printmaking at the RCA, were on the way back from a dinner (DCC?) and rather merry. ¶ They saw our cat, Rufus, a tough and battle-scarred ginger tomcat with only one eye, wandering down the road two streets from home in one of the squares. ¶ Berthold and Edwin cornered the cat and eventually managed to grab him after a struggle, and carried him home, telling him off for wandering so far and late. ¶ When Berthold got home, he set the cat down in the kitchen and fed and stroked him, and the cat purred as usual, and settled down to supper. At which point another one-eyed ginger tomcat, the real Rufus, walked in. ¶ Berthold said he did not know which of the three of them was more amazed, they all just stood staring at each other, which gave Berthold the chance to grab the fake Rufus, who seemed more resigned this time at being buttoned inside a coat, and carried him away apologising, back to the square, desperately trying not to look suspicious, or drunk, or be seen by anyone, especially not a policeman.

NICOLA DURBRIDGE I can almost hear it now—that rich German voice and the ready laugh. This was Berthold who had come with Deb to have a cup of tea and a piece of cake at my cottage. ¶ It was wonderful to have him there; it felt rather as if all of Europe was in my room as he talked, he had such encyclopaedic knowledge and wisdom, and shared it so easily with us all. And he was comfortable to be with too, like a kindly extra uncle.

ADRIAN BARTLETT There was a tap on my basement window one evening when I was printing a woodcut. It was dark outside and as I hadn't drawn the blinds my presses would have been visible from the street. A man in a voluminous jacket was gesturing to be let in. ¶ When I opened the door I recognised Berthold but he introduced himself anyway and asked me to excuse his curiosity about my printing presses. ¶ When quite young I had bought a copy of *The Studio book of Alphabets*, which included Albertus, so it was interesting to learn when we moved to Kennington that Berthold was a near neighbour. Up till now I had not yet spoken to him. ¶ We talked about presses for a while and what I was working on. He then plunged his hand into one of his many deep pockets and pulled out an enamelled metal object. ¶ I cannot remember now exactly what it was. Berthold said *'I've just bought this. I think its Byzantine. What do you think?'* I didn't know but said *'I'm sure you're right'*, *'Oh good, good'*, he replied. We chatted away for a bit, exchanged pleasantries, and he left.

ROWLEY ATTERBURY He worked at Fabers until his retirement, mainly on book jackets but sometimes on books, at which he excelled (usually after 4pm) his normal working hours being spent in second-hand book shops or junk shops of one kind or another. This was made possible by W.J Crawley, Faber Sales Director, who had to approve jackets, and who did not come to work himself until after 4pm. In between times Berthold collected ephemera of all kinds: writing instruments, books, paintings, lewis guns, nothing was too obsure for his collection. He also revived the practice of beachcombing along the banks of the Thames in the middle of London.

Encyclopaedia of World Politics

by Walter Theimer and Peter Campbell

BEST MOTOR RACING STORIES

with this block and without right out of register with (A)

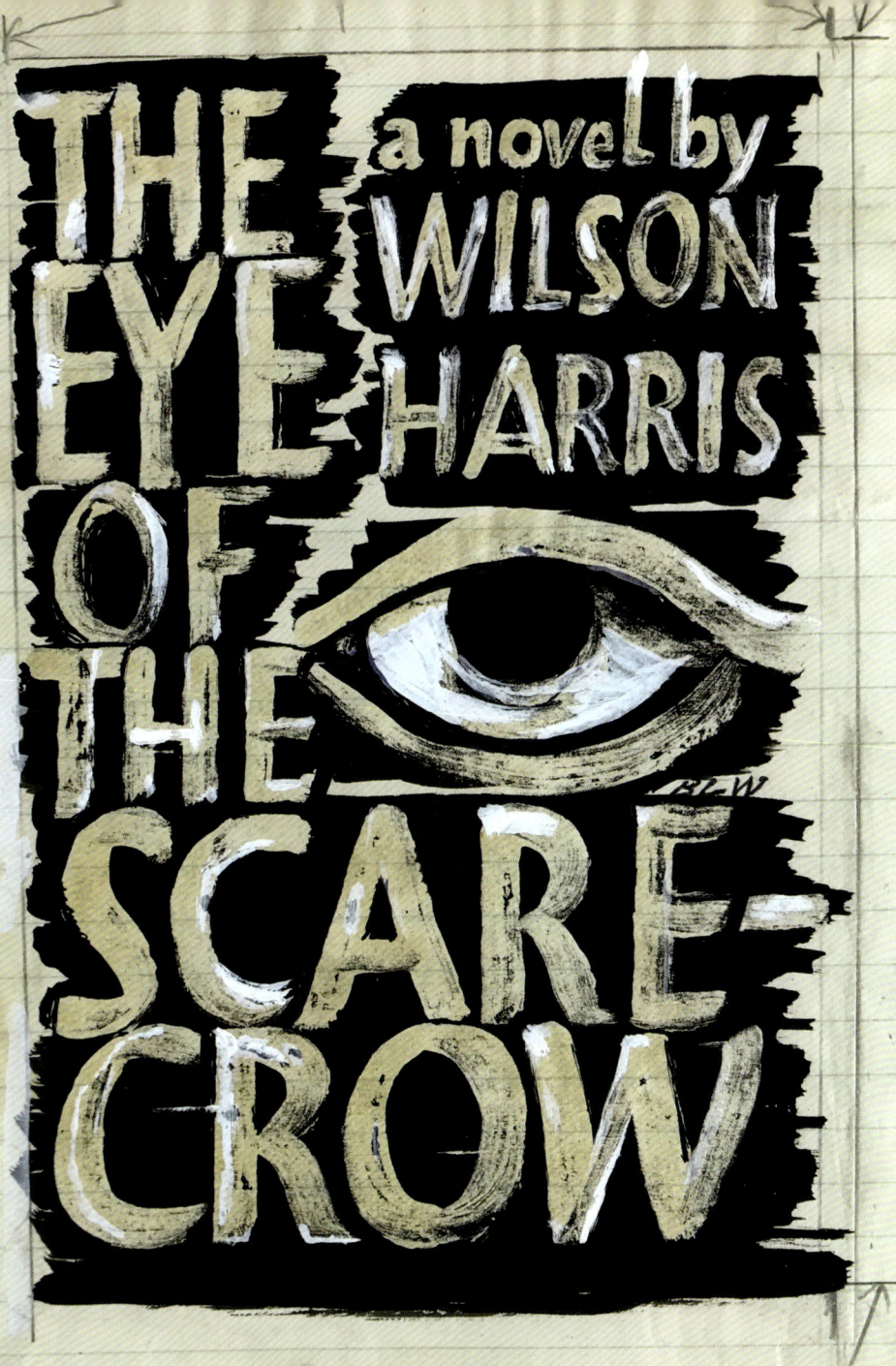

DHW Both Berthold and Margaret did the food shopping every day, as there was not much storage space in the old kitchen, and the gas refrigerator was referred to as the fermentator, as it was very inefficient, but still it kept the cat away from it's and our suppers. There was always a saucepan of soup on the stove, extended from day to day with whatever was on hand, there was very little wasted ¶ Margaret cooked every day, but Berthold almost always cooked the Sunday lunch, and breakfast for us when we were small and he was on holiday. ¶ Meal times were always cheerful, noisy, exciting occasions of great hilarity, which seemed to leave visitors slightly stunned. We all tended to talk at the same time, it seemed to work and no one minded, if you couldn't make your point you could always stand on your chair. If things got too out of hand, Berthold would say '*Don't get historical, it will end in tears...*' ¶ I remember one breakfast time Berthold cooking a huge omelette/frittata with only two eggs, plus milk, flour, onion and potato for the four of us, with just one single green pea in it (fished out of the soup?). We ate very carefully to find the hidden pea and be the lucky one. ¶ He used to quarter potatoes and roast them in their skins with garlic, salt, & olive oil and make little Yorkshire puddings in 12 compartment cake trays, two trays at a time. His speciality was rib of beef, which he would carefully buy with the bones in as it was much cheaper, and then bone and roll up with stuffing all tied up with string. ¶ He used a willow barrel shaped roller basket with a curved walking stick handle which he would wheel to the shops for food shopping but always carried an army surplus canvas satchel to work for books and papers. ¶ In the summer when the milk started to turn he showed us how to curdle it

with an old tarnished metal spoon, and leave it to drain overnight in a piece of muslin tied to the tap over a bowl, we didn't particularly like the cream cheese he made but the whey was okay added to the ongoing soup. ¶ All the vegetable peelings were kept and composted in the garden, where there was grown mint, rosemary (best avoided in cooking as the local fox population liked to roll on it), apples, soft fruit of all kinds, rhubarb, beans grown through the apple tree branches, peaches with thick furry skins (but delicious when peeled and stewed) and blackberries. ¶ Margaret was the gardener but Berthold liked to sit outside in the garden in the sun asleep with a newspaper, like the cat who would often sleep on the end of Berthold's bed, on his feet, making it difficult for him to turn over in the night. ¶ After cooking Sunday lunch he would try to read the Sunday papers on the kitchen table but it usually ended up as a fight with the cat who wanted to sleep on just the article Berthold was trying to read.

ROWLEY ATTERBURY He was one of the greats of the last century. Not for him a rehash of somebody else's work. His work was original both in thought and execution. Devices and ornaments of all kinds complemented his many type designs: Albertus, Pegasus, Hyperion, Decorata, Albertus Shadow and Sachsenwald to name a few. Albertus is well known, having been widely used, usually without acknowledgement. Pegasus, a little-used splendid text face for newspaper or book, so preferable to Times New Roman, was seen to advantage in Keith Murgatroyd's proposed Daily Telegraph redesign and in Berthold's own catalogue of his retrospective exhibition at the Victoria and Albert Museum. [*This book is also type-set in Pegasus*]

The Serpent

Neil M. Gunn

JERRY KELLY In the early 1980s I was with Berthold in New York once or twice. One of his visits coincided with that most American of holidays, Thanksgiving. I thought Berthold might enjoy a traditional Thanksgiving celebration, so I invited him to join my family and a gathering of friends and relatives assembled for Thanksgiving turkey in Queens, NY. ¶ One of my family friends had a son who was a little older than I and somewhat involved in design, working with handbag design and some television graphics. I introduced Berthold and mentioned that he was the designer of the Albertus typeface. Not only did my family friend know Albertus, he also said he liked the face very much and had used it a couple of times in his work. ¶ He was delighted to meet the designer, and Berthold was delighted that a chance event such as this would put him in touch with a fan from across the ocean.

SCW Berthold liked to improvise on the piano, or strum on a guitar. He sang one song which he said was from the Peasants' Revolt—the English version from 1381 was translated and sung in Germany in 1524—'*Als Adam grub und Eva spann, Wo war denn der Edelmann?*'. As small children we liked it when he sang '*Hoppe, hoppe Reiter, Wenn er fallt, dann schreiter. Fallt er in den Graben, Fressen ihn die Raben, Fallt er in den Sumpf, Macht der Reiter plumps!*' and bounced us on his knee.

SCW Berthold designed not only the jackets/covers for hardbacks and paperbacks, but also the lettering on the spines of clothbound hardbacks, so there is often a nice surprise to be found under the jacket.

VED MEHTA

WALKING THE INDIAN STREETS

FABER

DHW Late in the night if I crept downstairs to get a drink he would ask '*Who is there?*' and '*Go back to bed before you get cold.*' But if I asked to see what he was doing he would always show me what he was working on, and explain how it was done, and in the morning I would see the design tucked in to the hall mirror or on the mantelpiece, but always upside down so when he saw it in the morning he could look at it with fresh eyes. ¶ His workroom was full to bursting point and his desk was always covered with books and papers, with only a very small clear space to work on, when it got too badly silted up or the piece he was working on was larger than a book jacket, he would work on the kitchen table, the only partially clear space in the house ¶ Listening to his voice on tape recently I have remembered how precisely he spoke, but how slowly with lots of pauses (but not hesitations) which was infuriating if you were in a hurry or just wanted a short answer. ¶ The good thing about him was that even if it was late at night and he still had lots to do he would take time to talk and explain what he was doing and how it was done. I think that was why he was often late, time present was paramount?

GEORGE MACKIE One evening in his house I mentioned, the context I don't remember, that my mid-Victorian garden door lacked a knocker. Off he padded, silently, (did he always walk silently?) to return with a large cardboard box filled with an assortment of door knockers. ¶ It seemed he never passed a skip without investigating the contents.

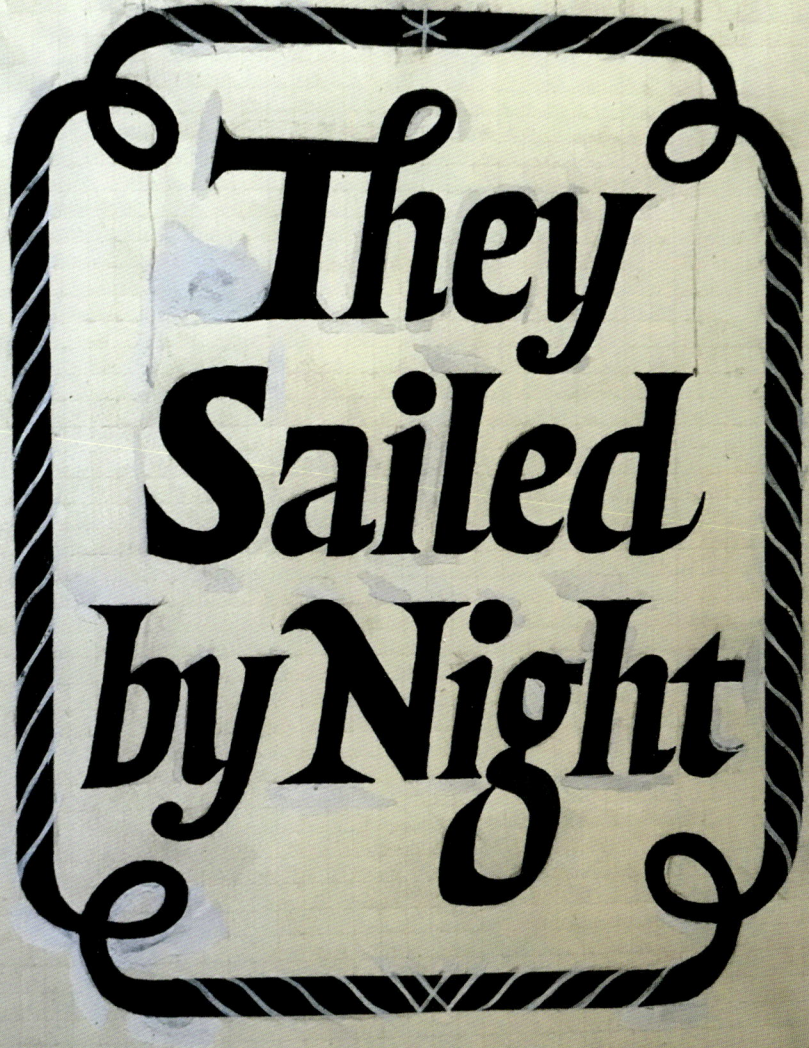

Drawing
1⅛" solid

author's name in sans in gold

square 1⅛"
SOLID

square (1⅛") solid

A Fly in Amber

HOPE-MIRRLEES

Solid squares to be blocked in RED with letters [TITLE] as shown
10⅛ (bold sans serif)

to be reversed only (not outlined in gold)

John Golding
C
U
B
I
S
M
Faber

(1/16" thick lines around the red square to be blocked in gold)

seven lines to be blocked in gold

1/16" thick

the other six lines (every space to be thinner about 1/32"

Faber in gold

1/8" solid

please return layout to B.L.W.

JERRY KELLY In the early 1980s I sublet Joseph Blumenthal's apartment in the Chelsea district of New York City. It had a spare bedroom, which I almost felt obligated to offer to visitors from out-of-town, since rooms are so scarce and expensive in New York. Once or twice Berthold stayed there with me, along with his wife. ¶ At that time (and probably still today) Chelsea was an enclave of the gay community. One night as Berthold, his wife and I were walking along West 21st Street a fellow in a leather vest, no shirt as I recall, leather pants, leather cap with a decorative badge, and spiked arm band walked by us. Berthold asked in all innocence '*Was that a policeman?*' I answered 'No.' then Berthold asked '*So who was that?*'. I instantly realized that if I said he was a gay man Berthold would probably ask me why a gay man would dress that way, and that was something I could not understand myself. I had to say '*Just skip it.*'

DHW I was asked to make a poster when I was at school, and Berthold showed me how to set it out like this: ¶ Work out roughly how many words and lines you'll need. ¶ Fold the paper horizontally for the number of lines of text plus one for the top space and one for the bottom space, (folded like a concertina). ¶ Fold in the sides to make margins the same as the top and bottom spaces, and then smooth it out, so you can see the folded margin and line spacing without the need for any pencil marks or measuring. ¶ Cut coloured paper strips the size of the page width minus the margins, but a bit narrower. ¶ Write the words on these strips, cut out the letters, arrange them within the folded margins till they look right, glue them down, and all the words will fit.

DHW On Sundays the whole family would climb in the blue Ford Thames van that Margaret drove and go to the bombed out area behind Whitechapel where there was a Sunday morning second hand market with the things to be sold laid on the ground or at best in cardboard boxes. ¶ I found some tiny stones with writing on them and showed them to Berthold. He was very excited and let me buy them explaining they were glass Tassie stones and had very fine lettering on them in reverse for use with sealing wax. ¶ At 1pm sharp the market closed and anything unsold and unwanted was set on fire, and we rushed into the nearby bakers to buy plum cheese cake, plaited onion rolls with black poppy seeds on top plus something for tea-time. ¶ Saturdays the van would take us to the Portobello Road market. Two of us children were meant to go with Berthold and the youngest, Toby, and one other was meant to stay with Margaret but we always wandered off and a lot of time was spent looking for each other. ¶ Berthold visited shops and stalls that had anything with writing on it, Margaret was looking for anything interesting and something for supper. Paul was fascinated by weapons of all types, and I looked for toys, Japanese things and small porcelain dishes. ¶ We would all despair if Berthold went anywhere with books as he would spend ages and not notice when we wandered off to find something else to do. ¶ As it got dark and the stalls began to close Margaret would slowly round up us children and then hunt Berthold down, it was always difficult to make him leave the market and come back to where the van was parked to go home for tea. ¶ Occasionally we would go to World's End Road market as there was a wider range of fruit and vegetables than in the shops locally. ¶ We

WHEN ALL IS DONE

Alison Uttley

The Chetniks
of Yugoslavia
by GEORGE SAVA

tried avocado pears from there for the first time, which were over ripe and black inside but we found them delicious eaten with oil & vinegar dressing. Also olives, which we all loved even if the two youngest ate them while squeezing up their eyes, Berthold told them they did not have to eat them if they did not like them, but they explained that they did like them, they just tasted a bit surprising. ¶ Once we were given a duck, which the fishmonger explained was only bad on one side. Margaret showed us how to pluck and clean it while Berthold made quill pens with the wing feathers. ¶ The most dramatic thing we tried was a tin of octopus legs in garlic sauce which we were all very keen to taste. We crowded around as the tin was cut open and when the lid was lifted off the little and very tightly packed legs uncurled out of the top and frightened us all, including Berthold & Margaret. ¶ Aunt Hilde, Berthold's sister, would visit once or twice every week and bring something from the continental delicatessen for tea. The thing we children liked most was a small Italian tin of vegetables in tomato sauce and olive oil. It also contained an anchovy fillet, with a pickled carrot strip, an olive, green beans, some cauliflower and other things we did not recognise. All of it had to be cut into 4 equal pieces to be shared out, I think Berthold only had the empty tin to extract the last smear of sauce from on a bit of bread. ¶ Aunt Hilde made a special hazelnut cake for important occasions, which Berthold loved. It was made with ground up nuts, bitter chocolate, lots of eggs, a little sugar and no flour. It was a family recipe and reminded them of their childhood holidays in the forests where their grandmother ran a saw mill and chain ferry in Russ, (then in East Prussia, now in Lithuania).

PETER GOLDSMITH My father was Berthold's first cousin. He always saw him when he came to London, and, indeed, before going to what is now Zimbabwe, in 1937, had a last meal with him, at Simpsons in the Strand. They decided to do the menu justice and eat for £1. They ordered generously and could not have eaten anything more by the end of the meal. ¶ The waiter was asked for the bill, and presented it, 19/6d. Gloomily they realised they had just failed, when the waiter returned apologetically and said he had brought them the bill for another table here was theirs—£1/0/6. Triumph. ¶ During the 1950s and 60's my father made a number of business trips to Europe, and on one occasion brought back a slim volume of drawings/cartoons celebrating Berthold. They showed him in his customary deer stalker and cloak, and I understood that he was not unpleased once when taking a cab to be asked '*where to, sir—221B Baker Street?*' ¶ So, as I travelled, coming to London in 1965, to visit the Wolpes at their Kennington home, I remarked to my father as we sat on the tube '*I think that is Berthold at the other end of the carriage*'. '*Nonsense*', said he, '*London is a huge place*'. ¶ But he looked and, sure enough, it was Berthold recognisable not only from his distinctive profile, but his hat and cloak ¶ Once left alone in London to go to university, Berthold was kind enough to invite me from time to time to join him and family or just him. ¶ I had begun to realise how uneducated I was in even the everyday of London's historical building and architecture and of the panoply of European art. ¶ I am deeply grateful to him, and his sister, Hilde, with whom I initially stayed, for their making manifest my deficiencies, and beginning an education that continues to this day.

Ambrose Heath
GOOD DISHES from TINNED FOODS
FABER

THE AMAZING STORY OF PETER, PAUL AND PERCY.
THE THREE PERKY PIGS!
BY MORLEY ADAMS

reduce to 1½"

One photostat neg.

Four & taken
R.L. Wolsee

STORIES FOR BOYS

B.S.
come
Direct

Please
loose the
pink
radiation

DAVID GENTLEMAN When I was about 17 my father gave me a copy of the *Shenval Press Handbook of Printing Types*, which for alphabetic reasons started with two pages of Albertus. So I knew about Berthold well before I met him. This was at the RCA in the fifties, where he was a visiting tutor in the graphic design school. He was shrewd and friendly: when a few years later Faber first asked me to illustrate a book about Suffolk, Berthold (then its design director) surprised me by hinting that Faber's fee was on the stingy side and that I could ask for a bit more. ¶ Throughout his years at Faber he gave a distinctive character to their jackets and insides. He was humorous and undidactic but he stuck firmly to whatever he minded about. ¶ At RDI discussions he would sit listening while everyone had their say, but he would then speak quietly and often carry the day. ¶ As calligrapher, type designer, typographer, pen collector and scholar with a European breadth of understanding. Berthold was a good person to have known.

SCW In the late 1950s Berthold became very ill, and went into St Stephen's Hospital in Fulham, where he was operated on by the surgeon who was Enid Blyton's husband, and was known to the medical staff as 'Noddy'. Our mother had to take all us children with her when she visited him, but as we were not allowed in, we had to sit on the steps outside and wait for her.

SUE SHAW Berthold did not care if you were man, woman or dog so long as you were interested in printing and lettering.

S.S. lineblock

Service Slang

collected by
J. L. Hunt and A. G. Pringle

illustrated by C. Morgan

Foreword by
Airmarshal Sir T. L. Leigh-Mallory

(spine: SERVICE SLANG • HUNT & PRINGLE • FABER)

DHW Berthold often used to work late into the night and I saw his light on and would creep down stairs to see what he was doing. Once he showed me what he called a wash-out. ¶ Earlier, the lettering had been painted in thick white watercolour on white paper, done very quickly, freely but precisely with a dryish brush, and not easy to see. ¶ When the paint was quite dry, Indian ink was brushed across it using a stiff brush leaving a few gaps towards the edges. Finally, when the Indian ink was dry, (and waterproof because of the shellac in it), the sheet was held under the bath tap and the white paint was washed out, taking some of the overlaying Indian ink with it, magically leaving the lettering in white against a black background. ¶ Berthold explained the most important thing was not to leave any Indian ink on the bath as it was difficult to remove and we would get in trouble!

PAULINE PAUCKER Berthold was so kind and so helpful and so enchanting and the house was like a treasure trove. ¶ When I first visited him he asked me if I would like a cognac. *'Isn't it rather early?'* I said (it was not yet 12:00 o'clock). He leant towards me, a kindly bear. *'My dear,'* he said, *'It is never too early.'* I think I accepted a liqueur chocolate. ¶ I was able to put in quite a few illustrations of his work in the piece I wrote on German-Jewish graphic artists for the Year Book of the Leo Baeck Institute in 1989, I think it's still online.

England
Herself

Rolf Gardiner

FIRST AID in AIR RAIDS

with a foreword by
Admiral Sir Edward Evans

6d net

2nd edition

by GEORGE SAVA

Surgeon's Symphony

separate here for colour

S.S. lineblock

separate here for colour

B.L. Wolpe

George Sava Surgeon's Symphony Faber

IAN CHILVERS I encountered Berthold twice. On both occasions he didn't speak to me but instead eyed me with great suspicion. I sensed that he viewed me as part of the 'new breed' at his beloved publisher, an upstart of whom he needed to be wary. ¶ In fact, the first time I saw him I didn't know who he was. He just appeared behind me and started tinkering with an old Adana Press that had been left in the Faber & Faber design department. I looked up from my drawing board (which in 1984 was the first to arrive at Faber's) and he stared at me between the platen, roller, gripper and the bed. ¶ I stared back at him and still remember thinking that his sideways head set against the Adana's inking disk was not unlike the depiction of a saintly figure in a Duccio composition. I concluded that this mysterious man must be of some importance. ¶ I briefly returned to my efforts to unblock my Rotring pen and when I looked again he'd vanished, just as silently as he'd appeared. ¶ This fleeting transcendental encounter over 30 years ago created a reverential aura around Albertus and it firmly placed the font in an exalted position in my mind.

APW I was offered a partnership in a nice GP practice in Fareham in 1987. One of the things the Surgery needed was a sign outside next to the road. I asked my father for his help. First of all, if you have access to talent then you should use it, but I also knew that it is easy to do these things badly and I did not want to mess it up. After all, I would be seeing the sign every day for the next 2 or 3 decades. ¶ Berthold said it should be simple. He suggested a size and then drew it out freehand. It was all terribly easy and natural. My

Hawksters Original Drawing

Best sf
SCIENCE FICTION STORIES

Best SF

SCIENCE FICTION STORIES
FABER   edited by Edmund Crispin
BLW

please do not loose the grey

line S.S

BLWolpe

NB best blah please if necessary make it on copper

Corporal JACK

David Scott

wife and I had gone up to London to see Berthold and Margaret. I asked about the sign and we then just cleared the kitchen table after dinner and Berthold did the sketches. ¶ Once he had drawn '*Surgery*', I then cut out his letters, transferring the paper cut-outs to a spare piece of vinyl bathroom floor covering. We stuck the individual vinyl letters onto a piece of plywood and finally glued on a mitred moulding as a border. I used car body filler to round the sharp angles where casting sand might hang up. When Berthold had done his lettering on bronze memorial plaques and church bells in the 1930's he would have used wax or clay for this. I had lots of car body filler in those days and it worked fine. In 1987 we still had a working iron foundry in the middle of Fareham The foreman took the finished and painted form and screwed a long threaded bar into the back. He tamped it down into the sand next to the drain covers and grids they were due to cast. He did this three times, twice for the two I needed and once for a spare, in case one did not cast successfully. ¶ Such was the founder's skill that all three signs came out fine. There are still two outside the Surgery. On the casting you can still see the tip of the screw end of the foundryman's rod where it came through the face of the form. It is just next to the top of the stem of the 'G'. ¶ I should have paid more attention and asked Berthold to explain more or teach me, but I was working very hard then and somehow felt that there would always be time for that later.

BLW I like teaching. I wouldn't be teaching if I didn't. I still teach just because I like to pass on skills and information.

SCW Berthold would reminisce about local foods in Hesse such as '*Handkase mit Musik*', and '*Lattwerch*'—a plum jam cooked for hours if not days, being stirred continually by a team of aunts and cousins. ¶ In 2005, when Deborah and I went to the Gutenberg Museum in Mainz for an exhibition of B's work, we were glad to see that '*Handkase mit Musik*' was still on the menu—a mild cheese shaped by hand to an oval shape (like a bar of soap)—and the '*Musik*' is pickled onions! ¶ Recently, I was pleased to find that '*Lattwerch*' is the jam bought by the Brave Little Tailor, in the Grimms' tale '*Das Tupfere Schneiderlein*'. Those relatives who made the jam all perished in the War.

RICHARD HOLLIS Wolpe was certainly a '*character*' at Fabers. He probably cultivated his exotic European-ness with his accent and curly-stemmed pipe. ¶ He worked more or less independently, on a different floor to the so-called '*book controllers*' who looked after the design and production. In design he was many-sided. His covers for the paperbacks were very different from the classical typography which he used on more elaborate books, such as Nicolete Gray's '*Nineteenth-Century Ornamented Typefaces*'. He surprised me by admiring the Perspex framing to a page of the '*Nuremberg Chronicles*' on the wall of our Holborn flat. ¶ He may have been suspicious of my '*gridnik modernism*' but was always very friendly. I used Albertus for headings in a Faber advertising leaflet and later discovered and used his Pegasus typeface for a John Heartfield exhibition guide. ¶ Berthold was a darling of several of the women working at Fabers. Gillian Chorley did a small celebratory book which you probably have, published in the 1960s.

Fishing Fortunes and Misfortunes

by G. D. Luard

Compost

for GARDEN PLOT or THOUSAND-ACRE FARM

a practical guide to modern methods

F. H. BILLINGTON

JULIA RAMOS The first picture in my mind is one of Berthold and Margaret, secondly of Berthold, Margaret and their children, thirdly of Berthold, the artist, designer and scholar, which covers a spectrum so wide and so brilliant that it is difficult to know where to begin. ¶ The earliest memories must go back to about 1961. My own family had moved to Lewes a few years before, and I already had 3 children, Julian, Tod and Ben. At the end of the school day my two older children would charge into the public gardens attached to Southover Grange. ¶ Very soon they met there and made friends with the four Wolpe children, Sarah, Deborah, Paul and Toby, who would arrive in Lewes for the holidays in a house in Lansdown Place nearby, but later the family moved to what must have been the oldest house in the street that Berthold (& Margaret) had bought in a derelict state, which they slowly repaired, restoring it with great care and judgement. Paul and Julian made particular friends with each other, sharing an interest in ancient weaponry, but all of them sharing fun, latest interests and discoveries. ¶ I would sit on the grass with Margaret and talk. Later Julian stayed with the Wolpes in London when they moved to a wonderful house in Kennington Park Road. Holidays in Lewes meant family expeditions to the sea, to Tide Mills and Cuckmere Haven. They usually brought back booty from the shore; driftwood, Second World War bits of armaments, shrapnel, glass washed smooth by the sea, lumps of chalk worn and pitted, resembling a Henry Moore maquette in miniature, and large bits of timber to be burnt on an open fire. ¶ After a visit to a local town Bertholds pockets would be stuffed with books & objects which sometimes only he could identify with his acute visual knowledge.

In those days, Sussex and indeed London was an open sesame of wonders. I remember him telling me he had found a shoebox full of beautiful flint arrowheads (at a street market in London) that he had named *'The Seven Dials Longbarrow Hoard'* since it was bought on a market stall there. ¶ I only realized the extraordinary scope of his achievement in so many different fields when I saw the exhibition of his work put on by the V and A in 1980. Especially it was good to see the huge array of book jacket designs he did for Faber. It was not just that they are beautiful and dynamic designs, but that each jacket reveals the essence of the author's work so clearly. Berthold & Margaret were people after my own heart; Margaret, so modest about her own beautiful work—which she continued to do throughout her life as well as being the most constant, balanced and optimistic soul—I never remember seeing her downhearted. ¶ Berthold had a streak of true genius, which was demonstrated not only in his inventiveness as a designer but by his scholarly and enquiring mind. Anything strange, unusual, be it an object found in a junk yard, or a box of craftsman's tools no longer used, would be a source for him, to re-assess and revalue what he had found. If one met him by chance he would retrieve such an object from his pocket and show you. His gentle sweetness and nobility showed always. He had worried concern but also great pride in his children's achievements. ¶ The Wolpes made such a difference to our lives in Lewes over so many years, and I miss Berthold and Margaret still.

DHW Berthold had been offered work in London but the work permit was slow in coming. While waiting for the papers he had been locked up by

TONY-PANDY

and other **RED** *poems*

IDRIS DAVIES
RED

The Green Isle of the Great Deep

Neil M. Gunn

the authorities in Offenbach for some days, with many other young Jewish men, and thoroughly frightened by the experience and the official behaviour and attitudes. The family then decided that it was no longer safe for him to stay in Offenbach and he had gone to Paris to see his Uncle, but could not afford to stay there very long. So he took a risk to see if he could get into England and hurry up the paperwork from within the country. ¶ He flew into Croydon Aerodrome but was stopped for not having the right papers. As there were no flights back to Paris that day and nowhere to hold him the police were sent for. ¶ By this time Berthold said he felt terrible, nervous and apologetic as he knew he was in the wrong. He was escorted to Croydon Police Station and put in the cells overnight. ¶ He told me he was amazed when a kind young policeman brought him some supper, a bottle of warm beer and an extra blanket, and explained that he was afraid the cell door had to be locked for the night as '*it was the regulations*' but wished him a good night's sleep. ¶ In the morning he was even more surprised to be given tea and porridge and greeted with '*Good morning, Sir, did you sleep well?*' before being taken back to the airfield. He said it made such a contrast with home and made him even more certain that coming to England was a good idea. He told me he admired Georgian architecture very much and thought anywhere that had such elegant and practical houses must be a decent place. As papers arrived within a few days of his being returned to Paris, he could at last leave mainland Europe and start a new life in London. ¶ The money he received for Albertus enabled him to bring his mother and sister to join him later, leaving Offenbach only weeks before the war broke out, so Albertus saved the family.

DHW Berthold and the four of us children would collect lead type from the ground in the lane outside Baxters the printers in Lewes. When we had enough he would show us how to cut moulds from cuttlefish shells, nice and dry, taken from the budgerigar's cage. The moulds were made, and the type melted in an old tin can on the gas cooker and cast into the hollows we had cut. ¶ He also made us lead '*marbles*' which we rolled along the floor for the cat to play with, that were cast in a handheld mould like a pair of pliers with a hollow centre that was actually for casting half inch bullets. ¶ I remember being shown how to cut the sprues off with the bullet caster and how hard the soft lead flashing around the ball was to cut with a knife. It was very exciting seeing the solid grey lead turn to molten silver when melted, and being able to make things from real metal. We had to be careful not to spill the hot lead on to the enamel top of the cooker, or worse still, on to the lino floor where it left little burnt tell tale holes. ¶ Another rainy day activity was making toys from thin plywood. We drew shapes on the plywood, or Berthold melted glue and stuck printed paper shapes (penny plain or tuppence coloured) on to the wood and then cut them out with a foot treadlled jigsaw. ¶ Berthold did it easily, but when I tried it was difficult to cut smooth curves and not to break the blade. '*Slowly! Slowly!*' he'd say, but too late! Still the shortened blade would be reset and the cutting continued.

SCW At home, the tall wooden stool which he sat on to work had a large india rubber attached to the top of the stool with a long length of string (so it could always be found easily) and couldn't be lost or '*borrowed*' by us children.

All Hallows Eve

Charles Williams

(spine): ALL HALLOWS EVE — CHARLES WILLIAMS — F&F

water & rain

the battle of aughrim

DHW Looking at a worse than usual school report Berthold asked, '*Did you really try hard? Yes?*', '*Well, always just try to do your best—and always be kind!*' Then, with a smile, '*Don't worry this will be forgotten about in a very short time*'. With a bigger smile '*If things get too bad you can always start again in another place!*'.

SCW On one occasion, having been irritated by some 'calligraphers' boasting of their £300 gold-nibbed Waterman pens, Berthold and Gunnlaugar SE Briem gave a demonstration of lettering using a dip-pen carved from a carrot, and a cigarette stub. This was to make the point that the tool itself was not important, but that each tool has its own characteristics, which must be discovered by experimenting, in order to make the best use of them.

DHW Berthold's grand-daughter, Nicola, about age three at the time, was very excited after being driven across Westminster Bridge to see the Coade Stone South bank lion standing up. She was certain that it used to lie down but, miraculously, it was now standing up. She started to get very upset when we wouldn't believe her. ¶ We tried to explain to her that she was probably confusing it with the Trafalgar Square bronze lions which we passed earlier in the year that are lying down. Nicola would not accept this, and it started to turn into a bitter argument. ¶ Berthold stopped us and said she was right, it was a miracle. He said that because she really believed in what she had seen, it was a miracle in the true sense of the word, and we were wrong to try and force her to change her mind.

ROWLEY ATTERBURY One evening, driving him to a Double Crown Club meeting on board the *Orsova*, prior to her maiden voyage from Tilbury, we were going through the City in the rush hour, when Berthold shouted 'STOP! STOP!', so I jammed on my brakes, a taxi ran into the back of my car and Berthold pointed to the Mansion House and said 'the largest sash window in London!'. The taxi driver was unamused.

E.M HATT His favourite time for enjoying a joke is five minutes after the teller's voice has died away. This is not to suggest that you will ever floor him with a question about the youngest maternal uncle of the Margravine of Styria, or the colour of Vautrollier's Sunday stock in his Edinburgh days.

SCW At the internment camp in Australia, in the large hut where Berthold slept, there was also a surrealist poet, who had gone into the desert and found a large poisonous spider, which he kept in a glass jar on the window-sill. ¶ BLW and the others in the hut disliked the spider being there because it made sinister shadows on the wall. ¶ So they wrote and posted up a notice saying that the Spider was to the Surrealist as a Budgerigar was to the Bourgeoisie. ¶ That comparison annoyed the poet so much that he took the spider back into the desert and released it.

DAVID GENTLEMAN When I mentioned Berthold at the RSA there was a sort of rustle of delight at the thought of him...

The Swinger

Gunby Hadath's
new school story

If their Mothers only knew

DHW On returning to London from 10 months internment in Australia Berthold had nowhere to live. With the help of friends he moved into an empty room in the Middle Temple as all legal papers and personnel had been evacuated to the safety of the country leaving the chambers completely empty. He said it seemed very strange being the only inhabitant of such ancient chambers overlooking beautiful courtyard gardens in the heart of the City, surrounded by trees and falling bombs. ¶ During the night, staff at Fabers took turns on the roof fire-watching. Berthold told me he was nervous to find he was to share the watch with his boss, but when offered a swop with Margaret, (they married soon after), T.S Eliot readily agreed and Berthold found her much more attractive and congenial company! ¶ Of all the things Berthold heard and saw during this time he said one of the most awful was a piano, in flames, falling slowly through several floors of a burning building. He told me it seemed to him like the sound of the end of civilisation. ¶ One morning when Berthold arrived at Russell Square for work, he found the whole place cordoned off and full of officials, who were very excitedly searching the gardens around a large bomb crater. The rumour was that they had found the remains of a very unusual bomb. When the gardener saw the mess he was very upset, and complaining bitterly that all his gardening tools had been totally destroyed, even his especially large, iron lawn roller. At this point all the cordons were removed, the square was reopened and Berthold went into work. ¶ Berthold, who loved unusual heavy iron objects, had this piece of shrapnel on his desk as a paper weight, (and memento mori?) As a child I liked to think it was part of that lawn roller.

ANNET STIRLING I was one of the first year intake of students on the new Lettering Diploma Course at the City and Guilds of London Art School. It was set up—as far as I remember—because Berthold lived very close to the college and Roger de Grey, the principal at the time, was quite interested in lettering. The college already had a flourishing signwriting workshop run first by William Sharpington and then by his pupil Bob Duvivier, the latter also taught on the new course. ¶ Monday was Wolpe day. Berthold would come in with books from his library and would proceed to tell us about an historical letter form, showing pictures in the books as he talked. The books were tantalising but '*hoof prints*' were forbidden, we were allowed to watch but not touch. ¶ After this he would bring out some flat/broad brushes and other interesting things from his capacious pockets and paint the alphabet he had been talking about. We all watched carefully and spent the afternoon practising. Some people might call this calligraphy, but to us it was brush lettering! ¶ As students we were surprised but pleased to see Berthold at the Christmas School Party that year, generally having a good time and dancing with all the students. Tutors were not really supposed to attend, and Berthold was already quite a venerable age. ¶ He never came to any others, and I recently found out from Deborah, his daughter, that he did his back in whilst dancing, and did not receive much sympathy from the medical profession—as he was not supposed to dance at his age! How times have changed…

SUE SHAW Berthold was never boring, being consistent is boring, consistency is over rated.

S. S. lineblock

The Beautiful People
AND OTHER PLAYS

(spine) The Beautiful People

Sword of Bone

Anthony Rhodes

Faber & Faber

VIC COOK I met Berthold Wolpe in his house in Kennington due to my knowing his son in law and daughter. There I was, a young packaging designer trying to come to terms with the new age of computer typesetting and sitting in the kitchen of this legend of typographical design, partaking of toast and tea that he had kindly made for me while I waited for my friends. ¶ We had a most interesting discussion on the subject that he is renowned for, concerning the benefits and pitfalls of the new technologies which both of us from different generations were coming to terms with. I must confess that this first meeting left me in complete awe. His attitude was enquiring but genial, obviously wanting to embrace knowledge on anything concerning typographical design and its uses. ¶ We met a number of times after this initial meeting and his openness and humility always impressed me and I am sincerely thankful that I had the opportunity to obtain a little insight from, in my humble opinion, a genius whose legacy is still with us and which can be seen today almost everywhere if we look.

JOHNNY GUMB My sisters and I have warm memories of Berthold, and of course these often come to life when I talk to Sue Shaw, down the road at The Type Archive. I always remember my father, Alex Gumb, telling us how Berthold worked on type designs in the flat which they shared (in Bayswater?). ¶ Apparently the Monotype Corporation had agreed to pay Berthold a certain amount for each character, so with my father's encouragement, he continued to produce designs for as many extraneous characters as they could think of!

ELLIC HOWE When Berthold had returned from internment in Australia he was free to work and settled in London, and was about to marry Margaret, whom he had met before the war in Chelsea at a tea party held by William Oley for art students and refugee artists, (both went partly for the company and partly for the free tea and cakes, according to Margaret). ¶ The day before their marriage he was summoned in great secrecy to a hotel in the West End, and asked by Ellic Howe of the Secret Operations Executive, (S.O.E), to design a subversive New Year card in German blackletter to be printed and used to annoy the Gestapo. ¶ Berthold was more than happy to do anything to frustrate the Gestapo but explained that he would not be able to start on the design that night as he was getting married the very next morning. ¶ In his book, the Black Game, Mr Howe writes that when the urgency was explained to Berthold he agreed to do the design immediately, but Berthold told me that he was told that he would not be getting married if he did not complete the design that very night, and he was not sure what powers the department had, or what they intended so he desperately worked all night, delivered the drawings and was allowed to marry Margaret as planned and hoped for.

BLW Type is not just type. People talk about type in a very general fashion, therefore lots of arguments start which are quite unnecessary if you'd made it quite clear in the beginning whether you are talking about a display type or a reading type.

ALAN KITCHING Sometime in the 80s I commissioned Berthold to execute a piece of calligraphy. It was to address an envelope for the Queen Mother. I remember he gave a wonderful swash to the tail of the capital Q. ¶ But the memory I have most was when I offered a knife and straightedge for him to cut down the sheet of paper he was using. He turned to me and said *'Never cut paper when you can tear it'*. Ever since, to this day, I always tear.

SCW When Berthold's daughter Deborah & her husband Jock came back from Japan in 1975, Deborah found work as a potter's assistant to Geoffrey Eastop (who worked with John Piper at Fawley Bottom Farm), and Jock taught woodwork at a tough inner London school, staying with Berthold and Margaret in Kennington. ¶ Berthold, believing strongly in the importance of teaching and learning, made an informal arrangement with the City & Guilds Art School where he taught lettering, whereby he would teach unpaid on Mondays in exchange for Jock's fees on the one year Post Graduate carving and gilding course. ¶ On finishing this year Jock got work in the framing department of the National Gallery, which set him up for his later career.

BLW I've actually used Albertus quite a lot myself on book jackets for one reason it is quite economic and does not run wide. The economy of design is an important part of type design and particularly to save a lot of line space.

SCW One Christmas Berthold came home to find the fig tree in their front garden had been decorated by his lettering students from The City and Guilds Art School. ¶ It was hung all over with strips of different coloured paper with words such as *'Peace', 'Noel', 'Pax', 'Alleluia'*, etc. written in different lettering styles. ¶ That term the students had been doing a project with him based on *'Weathergrams'*—work originally devised by US calligrapher Lloyd J Reynolds, who wrote haiku-type poems in Indian ink on strips of brown kraft paper and hung them from trees. ¶ This project had caught the students' imaginations—Berthold was very pleased and touched by their tribute.

JTW When people reminisce about my father, they often mention his appearance. The pipe, Donegal tweed hat, and the then unfashionable shoulder bag for books and other new acquisitions. They also recall his humour and softly spoken manner, but what did he sound like? ¶ I had a shock recently when I heard a 1980s recording of him addressing students in America. His accent was far more German than I'd remembered. As children, we almost never heard him speak German at home because of his experiences in the Nazi era. When he occasionally woke at night shouting, my mother would brush it off with, '*He thinks they're coming for him.*' ¶ Eventually, he did help with German homework, and we also talked together in German to practise for my A Level. I was even told later that my German had acquired some of his Hessian inflections, but when I was young it never occurred to me that he sounded anything but just Berthold. ¶ As a child, I once lost him in a museum—easily done with my father. When

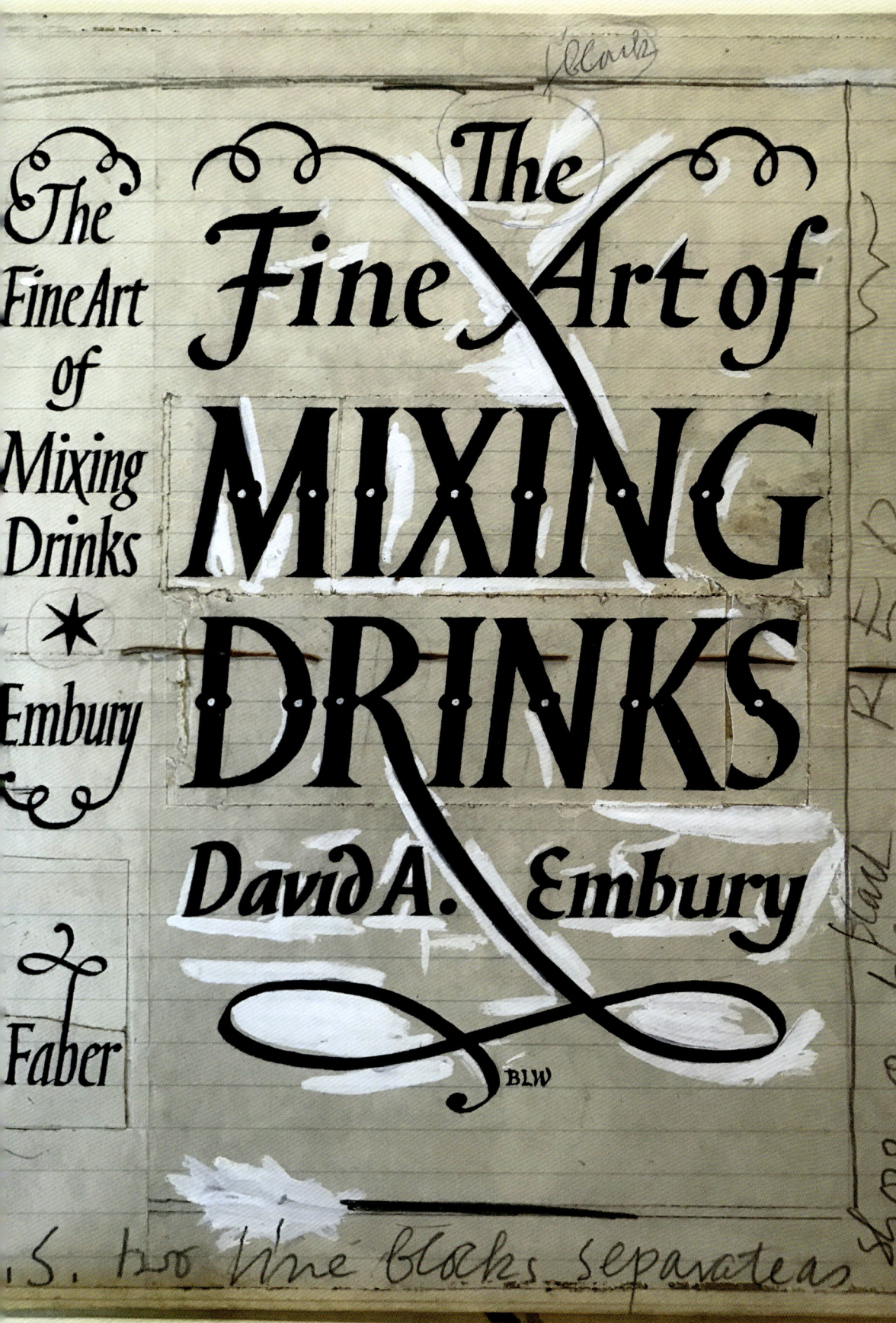

I asked at the front desk if they had seen him, the woman said, '*Do you mean the gentleman with the German accent?*' Without a second's thought, I said, '*No*', and had already turned away before I realised she was talking about dad.

BLW Modern electronic methods are only tools for reproducing something. ¶ Photo type setting is probably hurting typography only through the fact that people don't know the basic conditions and rules of design. I think if the design is right you can produce it on anything. ¶ These are only systems on which any kind of type can be produced. It's not only lettering, it is aesthetics, it is legibility, you see, and style. ¶ Well, I don't think anything has changed, because the curious thing is the Roman capitals we use were created 2000 years ago and they look quite modern, I mean, this A or this L, they haven't changed. ¶ They are so simple that they are still modern, and you can find some Roman inscriptions of the Republican period which even have sans serif lettering as they didn't use serifs at that time.

CHARLES SHEARER It is really only a memory of seeing Berthold at the City and Guilds of London Art School in the mid 1980s. It was just a glimpse of a classroom with Berthold in the centre, surrounded by students who were all engaged in lettering exercises with pieces of chalk on sheets of slate.

ROWLEY ATTERBURY Another time, after working in the Press, we put him on the 705 Green Line bus for London. He apparently left the bus at the first stop and in the morning he was to be seen fast asleep on our front lawn, covered in frost—it was January after all! He also designed and cut the gravestone for my dear dog Chippy, helped by Charles Mozley.

SCW Berthold used Cow Gum, a petrol-based rubber glue, to paste up his artwork. It stayed fluid for a very short time, which allowed minor adjustments to be made—& lumps of the dried rubber could be used for cleaning up edges. ¶ Over time, B had collected up a large, tennisball-sized lump which he kept on his desk. One day, when we were visiting him in his office at Faber & Faber, he picked up the ball of Cow Gum, and, laughing, threw it at the window! It bounced off and ricocheted around the room. ¶ As children, we were always terrified that something would get broken by accident, so it was very alarming to see something deliberately thrown at a window.

ROWLEY ATTERBURY Berthold was a modest, warm man and a great supporter of younger people starting enterprises in the graphic fields. Somewhat fondly mocked by the satirical drawings of Charles Mozley and dressed like Sherlock Holmes, he was greatly underrated. He may be gone but his work will live long after the current rehashed inferior type designs are forgotten.

THE TILTED CROSS

S.S.
line
sharp
black
please

ETA INGHAM LAWRIE While living in Offenbach am Main, Germany, my parents were friends with Berthold and his sister Hilde. Berthold, teaching and working with the calligrapher Rudolf Koch at the Offenbach Art School, introduced my father to gold and silver smithing which became his chosen vocation. ¶ In the 1930's the Wolpe family managed to emigrate to England. We were evacuated during the war, shortly after my father died, and contact was lost. Hilde managed to reconnect with my mother and their friendship was rekindled. Visits to and from England and Germany followed. ¶ As a teenager I visited London for the first time on my own, staying with Hilde and visiting Berthold, his wife Margaret and their lively young family in their home in Kennington. A house like no other: Every nook and cranny full of unusual and rare objects, the walls lined with books, so much so that the floors began to sag! ¶ Later as a 'foreign' student at the RCA I experienced Berthold as a designer and teacher, encouraging and correcting but always with a twinkle in his eyes. It was good to know him.

ROWLEY ATTERBURY Decorata, a personal gift to me, rarely seen, is a decorated type in the best tradition and will no doubt follow Ian Mortimer's superb present work, when he arrives at contemporary decorated typefaces.

Opposite Decorata *typeface was first used on the* Great Flower Book, *designed by Ruari McLean, who wrote the obituary at the front of the book. His alphabet of foilated letters was subsequently completed as a personal gift to Rowley Atterbury's Westerham Press. Kindly lent by Rowley's son, Francis.*

THE ENTERPRISE
of England

Thomas Woodrooffe

Dear Baby

WILLIAM SAROYAN

Wohlauf Kameraden!

↑ This cover not for reproduction.

APW I found a Nazi song book when I was going through my father's papers. A lot of people who were young in Germany in the 1930's would have had things like that and many of their children and grandchildren will have come across these things and wondered about them. ¶ My father was the typographer and designer Berthold Wolpe. He had lost his job, teaching in an art school, because he was Jewish. He was no longer to be allowed to pollute the culture of the Reich. There was some family history of doing that. In the 18th century his grandfather's grandfather had been entertaining the citizens of Offenbach with woodcuts of newsworthy events, such as the execution of Marie Antoinette.
¶ I could not think why he had this book and then I found yet another copy. This one had some pencil notes and measurements on one of the decorations, a very nicely done eagle. From 1941 my father's typographic skills and German background had been employed by the P.W.E (Political Warfare Executive) in their production of propaganda and I thought that perhaps he had been taking the image of the eagle to use in one of these projects.
¶ Monotype has just relaunched 5 of Berthold's Type faces and I was going through his artwork looking for things relevant to the exhibition they were planning.' Whilst doing this I came across Berthold's original Drawings for the title of '*Wohlauf Kameraden*' and the five decorations that

:29th:April:1936:
:55th:Dinner:

DCC

Double Crown Club 74 : 27 October 19

appear in the book. He has written '*this cover not for reproduction*' so I am going against his wishes here. Booksellers state that the decorations are by Rudolf Koch, Berthold's mentor and teacher but they are not; they are Berthold's. I can only think that Rudolf Koch's Werkstatt (the Craft studio in Offenbach) passed the commission on to Berthold at a time when he was barred from working. Rudolf Koch died in 1934 and Berthold always said he owed him a huge debt of gratitude for help and advice and perhaps for things like this too. Koch's son Paul was also a fine craftsman and took over the Werkstatt. He disappeared on the Eastern Front in 1943. ¶ I can understand why my father was not proud of this commission but I think that this is worth reporting. The song book that was meant to inspire the young Nazis was beautifully decorated by an artist who was prevented from working because he was Jewish. The song book, Rudolf Koch, his kindness to my father and what happened to Rudolf Koch's son are all human stories that underlie this period of history. Also, if anyone has bought a copy of the songbook because they still think that National Socialism is a good idea, I hope that this piece, in some kind of a way, disarms the book and makes it just a good joke.

Opposite In Berthold's time, the Double Crown Club (DCC) met for their dinners and talks at Kettners restaurant, just off Leicester Square. The serviette is yet another example of Charles Mozley drawing on anything that came to hand, this time with his lithography pencil. The crown of open books was designed for a dinner menu, printed by Foister and Jagg of Cambridge. A reduced size of this was used on the note-paper of the DCC club's secretary in 1947. *Overleaf verso* Shown is Berthold's handwriting from when he lived in Germany, his handwriting when he moved to England and an example of the handwriting he adopted when he played the hand of Shakespear in the 1970 BBC television show. *Overleaf recto* This letterform is from one of the numerous large teaching alphabets, used at the RCA and the City and Guilds Art School.

BADISCHE KUNSTGEWERB[E]

Zuname: Wolpe
Vorname: Berthold Ludwig
Beruf: Zeichner
Geburtstag: 29. Oktober 1905
Geburtsort: Offenbach/M
Staatsangehörigkeit: Hessen

very sincerely yours,

Berthold L. Wolpe

Wm Shappero & Anna w[...]

Wm Shappease and Anna

TEMPEST TITLING

DESIGNED BY BERTHOLD WOLPE
AT THE FANFARE PRESS

FRESH & BOLD
ABCDEFGHIJKL
MNOPQRSTUV
WXYZ =-,:·!?

DEFGHIJ
ORUVW
56789
LCADE

LOUIS
Golding's
NEW NOVEL
THE
PURSUER

FANFARE ORNAMENTS Ernest Ingham, the founder of the Fanfare Press, persuaded Berthold Wolpe to supplement the conventional fleurons with modern designs. With this commission in mind, Wolpe designed a series of type ornaments from 1935 onwards. A selection of these was cut in 1936 and matrices were struck from which a supply was cast. In this book, Wolpe composed the units into borders, patterns and decorative tail-pieces and made them up into pages. The entire book, with the Tempest type used on the title page, is his own design and it was completed by Christmas 1938, but only a unique copy bears this date. ¶ From James Laver's introduction: '*Yet the little bits of metal which are the notes of the printer's keyboard can be cut to many shapes, and there is no reason why their number should be arbitrarily limited to twenty-six, or to fifty-two, plus comma, colon, and full-stop...yet there is no reason why he should not sometimes take a holiday and amuse himself with printable projections on metal which are decorative units and nothing else.* ¶ *'Where shall he find such decorative units? Shall he go back to the printers' ornaments of earlier ages, or shall he employ an artist (one who understands typography and finds a volupté in the very smell of printers' ink) to devise for him new shapes with which to construct new patterns?'* ¶ The device at the top of the page was drawn into a computer and used to form the patterned end papers throughout this book, in colourways inspired by Berthold from the 1940–50s.

Opposite *Tempest Titling was cut for Ernest Ingham for the exclusive use of the Fanfare Press, he said of the type. 'The curves to the horizontals... add a sense of movement and a feeling of urgency'.*

DHW On moving to London, Berthold changed the style of his handwriting from German script to Italic. It is interesting too that he didn't speak German at home in London, even to his sister, he seems to have put his German life behind him.
¶ The building where the Wolpe family lived in Offenbach was returned to Berthold when the war ended. A few years later, without telling Margaret, he gave it away to the neighbours on each side so they could sell it and raise cash to repair their roof which was leaking due to bomb damage. He had no aparent interest in his old house by then. ¶ Also after the war ended Berthold did not apply for a reparation pension. The family joked that as the tribunal only sat for 25 years he did not have enough time to get around to filling in the forms, but I don't think he wanted to do it, maybe he felt he had moved on and was immersed in life in England. ¶ On being awarded a discretionary pension anyway by the town of Offenbach, Berthold didn't use it (or declare it for tax in either country!) but left it for Margaret.
¶ I feel all these actions/inactions show the conscious effort he made to start a life in England, and he was delighted to receive recognition here like the RDI and OBE, and design mastheads for institutions like The Times, The Jewish Chronicle, Girl & Eagle, as well as being able to teach the next generation here and pass on his enthusiasms, which he enjoyed doing greatly.

Opposite The mastheads designed by Berthold Wolpe. Logos for Eagle and Girl published by Hulton Press, first appeared in 1950 and 1951 respectively.

The Jewish Chronicle

THE ORGAN OF BRITISH JEWRY

One Hundred and Fifth Year

No. 4,038.
Regd. as a Newspaper

INCORPORATING THE "JEWISH WORLD"
Established November 1841

Friday, August 30, 1946—Ellul 3, 5706

Price: 4d.

ROUND-TABLE TALKS

Will the Mufti be Invited?

The Foreign Office has announced that the London Conference on Palestine will open on September 9.

Invitations for this date have been sent to the Governments of the Arab States, the Jewish Agency for Palestine, and to the Arab Higher Executive for Palestine.

The Jewish Agency was officially invited on August 15 by the British Government, to take part in the proposed round-table talks. A spokesman in Jerusalem announced on Sunday Dr. Weizmann wrote a letter to Mr. George Hall, the Colonial Secretary, stating that the Jewish Agency could not take part in any talks on the basis of the proposals outlined by Mr. Herbert Morrison in the House of Commons. The letter went on to demand full freedom for the Jewish Agency to name its own delegates, including any persons who were detained or who might be detained in the future.

The Agency, it was urged in the letter, should invite, in consultation with His Majesty's Government, all the members of the Jewish delegation, on the understanding that representatives of other important Jewish bodies and organisations would be included.

A Jewish Agency statement on the invitation to

JEWISH AGENCY POLICY

Solution Must be Based on Statehood

The following statement by the Jewish Agency Executive was released in Paris on Friday last:

"The Executive of the Jewish Agency for Palestine was in session in Paris from August 2 to August 20. Members from Palestine, Great Britain, and the United States participated. Dr. Chaim Weizmann, President of the Jewish Agency, was prevented through ill-health from attending, but continuous contact was maintained with him, throughout the meetings. Mr. David Ben-Gurion, Chairman of the Executive of the Jewish Agency presided. At the first meeting, a message of greeting and solidarity was sent to the members detained in Latrun by the British Government.

"The whole situation of the Jewish people and Zionism was reviewed in the light of reports submitted on Palestine, European Jewry, Great Britain and the United States. The deliberations were conducted in the shadow of the deepening Jewish tragedy in Europe and the grim events in Palestine.

"The Executive condemned the continuation of the White Paper Policy by the Mandatory Power, its recent acts against the Yishuv, and the naval, military, and political blockade launched against Jews seeking a haven of refuge in their National Home. It considered this policy to be a flagrant

FORCING THE JEWS OUT

Polish Terrorist Methods

[From our Correspondent—WARSAW]

Some of the few Polish Jewish Communities in the smaller towns have tried to stay on, but have found it impossible to stand out against the threats of death from the N.S.Z. (the underground, anti-Semitic nationalist organisation). What happened in Zamosc is typical of the methods employed by the Polish terrorists.

Zamosc is an ancient town and takes its name from Count Zamoyski, who founded the town in the middle ages, when Jews first settled there. I. L. Peretz, the famous Jewish poet and writer, was born there in the second half of last century. The town was well known in Poland as a centre of Jewish learning, particularly of progressive learning.

The Jewish Community there numbered about 10,000, among whom were some widely-known Jews, landowners, millers, and manufacturers, whose families had been settled there for generations.

The Germans liquidated the Jewish Community in 1942. Very few escaped. Those who did, went to Russia and returned hoping to settle down again. They found their houses, shops, factories, and land in non-Jewish hands, and they were not even allowed to enter, much less take possession of them. When some insisted, the Christian owners found

UNION OF RELIEF BODIES

Organisations to Combine Appeals

By an agreement reached at a meeting on Monday evening, the Jewish organisations in this country presently engaged in the work of overseas relief, as the whole or part of their activities, have united to make one appeal.

They are the Federation of Jewish Relief Organisations and its affiliated bodies, such as the Polish Jewish Relief Fund, the Federation of Polish Jews, the Association of Baltic Jews, and others; the Chief Rabbi's Religious Emergency Council; British Ort; British Ose; the Agudist relief bodies, including their Foreign Relief Department and the Keren Hatorah; and the Mizrachi relief bodies, including the Bachad and the Mifal Hatorah. The Vaad Hayeshivot is also believed likely to join, as far as its work of providing food and clothing for refugee Rabbis and students is concerned.

This union, which has been largely brought about by the help and encouragement of the Board of Deputies, was initiated at a meeting of the Council of the Federation of Jewish Relief Organisations a few weeks ago, when a letter from Professor S. Brodetsky was read, in the course of which he said:

ACKNOWLEDGEMENTS This book would never have been possible without the huge amount of work undertaken by Berthold's family, plus the help of The Type Archive. ¶ Thank you to all the members of The Double Crown Club who sent in their anecdotes, which helped show a real insight into Berthold's life and filled this book. ¶ To Francis Atterbury for use of his father's text and the supply of printing blocks; Berthold's great friend Sue Shaw, for the use of text from *Wolperiana: An illustrated guide to Berthold L. Wolpe* and the use Charles Mozley's drawings. ¶ To Lynne Alexander and Sarah Harrison from The Lettering Arts Trust for putting on the exhibition of *Berthold Wolpe: The Total Man*, which instigated this book; Michael Barrett at The Press Office, who has lent us his PR talents. ¶ To Lauren Millwaters for all her design work on this project, Yihong Huang for patiently colouring the endpapers and Jennifer Penny for all prepress work. To John Byrne, thanks for saving us from last minute clunks. To Dave Davies from DLM Creative and Hartgraph for producing such a fine book.

Opposite The masthead for The Jewish Chronicle 1946 designed by Berthold Wolpe.

PROF. PHIL CLEAVER *The Author is a multi-award winning designer, who sees things differently. Protégé of Anthony Froshaug, Phil honed his design and typographic skills under Alan Fletcher, Wim Crouwel, and Michael Wolff. ¶ Alongside running et al design consultants, started in 1992, he is a Professor in the Creative Industries at Middlesex University, London, a Visiting Professor of typography at Birmingham City University and a Fellow of Hereford College of Arts. ¶ Phil is a founding trustee of The Monotype Type Museum, a board member of the International Type Academy, and a Fellow of both the Chartered Society of Designers and the Royal Society of Arts. He is also Artistic director to The Type Archive. ¶ His reputation is such that his early typographical work is archived in St Bride's Printing Library and his book design is in the permanent collection of the Victoria and Albert Museum's National Art Library. ¶ He wrote and designed the international best seller:* What they didn't teach you in design school.

The Lettering Arts Trust

The Lettering Arts Trust marks its 30th anniversary this year. The charitable trust champions excellence in the lettering arts by fostering talent, extending knowledge and facilitating new works. ¶ It is the UK's leading voice for promoting lettering to public and professional audiences. It brings the finest artists and the public together through training programmes and apprenticeships, events and exhibitions and original commissions. Based at Snape Maltings, our permanent gallery showcases the work of renowned lettering artists, while our shop displays the work of today's leading contemporary makers. The Lettering Arts Trust is also a custodian of the 'Art & Memory' Collection of contemporary lettered works held at various sites around the country.

Portrait by Lawrence Gowing.

 *The drawings of Berthold Wolpe used through the book and cover are by Charles Mosley who enjoyed drawing Bertold on any thing that came to hand, from scrapes of paper to fire doors. The one above was used the Frankfurt Book Fair Catalogue, printed by Rowley Atterbury in 1956.*

Published in 2018 by Impress

Impress
Editorial Department [156]
95 Wilton Road
London, SW1V 1BZ

Copyright—2018.
All rights reserved.

No part of this publication may be reproduced, transmitted, or stored in a retrieval system, in any form, or by any means, without permission in writing from the author. This book is sold subject to the condition that it shall not, by way of trade or otherwise, be lent, hired out, resold, or otherwise circulated without the author's prior consent in any form of binding or cover other than that in which it is published, and without a similar condition being imposed on the subsequent purchaser.

Copyright restrictions in favour of the BLW estate apply © 2018

The moral rights of the BLW estate have been asserted.

ISBN 978 1 9997825 4 2

www.impress-publishing.com

Designed by Prof. Phil Cleaver and Lauren Millwaters of et al design consultants.
Typeset in Monotype's Albertus Nova and Wolpe Pegasus.
Print production by Dave Davies of DLM Creative.
Printed in England by Hartgraph.

Corrigendum: an error in a printed work discovered after printing and shown with its correction on a separate sheet.

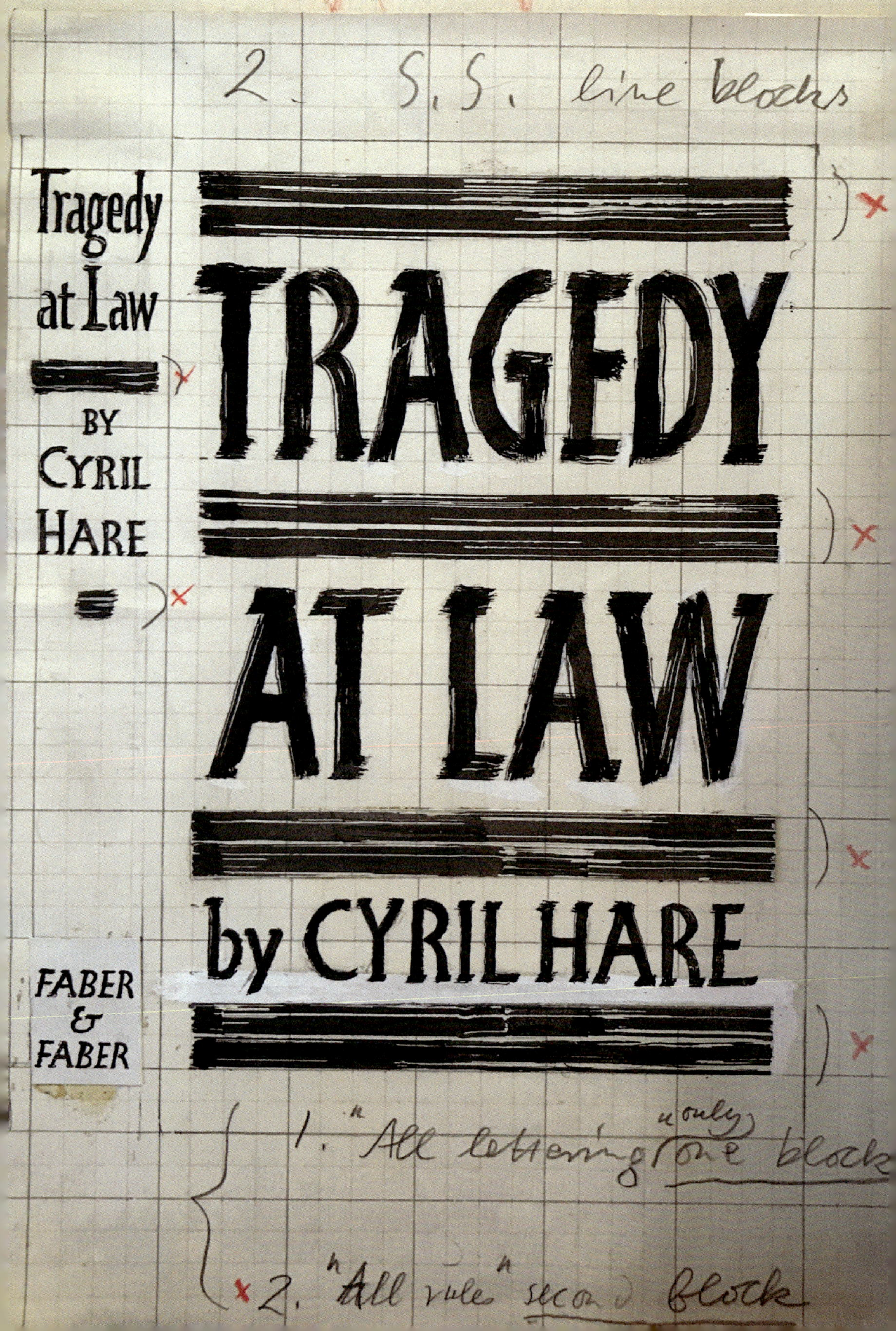

2. S.S. line blocks

Tragedy at Law

BY CYRIL HARE

TRAGEDY AT LAW

by CYRIL HARE

FABER & FABER

1. "All lettering" (only) one block

2. "All rule" second block

		Original	Correction
page	5	any-thing	anything
	7	*Bethold's*	*Berthold's*
	9	*Obituary of Berthold was*	*Obituaries of Berthold were*
		Author	author
	11	*friend advised*	*friend, advised*
		onto	*on to*
	23	*monotypes*	*Monotypes*
		royal designer for industry	Royal Designer for Industry
		Designer—Craftsmen	Designer-Craftsmen
	27	*first*	delete *first*
	28	photgraphically	photographically
	40	based those	based on those
		monotype	*Monotype*
	119	*foilated*	*foliated*
		was subsequently completed	*was completed subsequently*
	125	*Shakespear*	*Shakespeare*
		Guilds Art School.	Guilds of London Art School.
	130	aparent	apparent

The drawings of Berthold Wolpe used throughout the book are by Charles Mozley, who enjoyed drawing Berthold on anything that came to hand, from scraps of paper to a fire door. This drawing was used for the Frankfurt Book Fair Catalogue, printed by Rowley Atterbury in 1956.